A HISTORY OF
DARTMOUTH
BIBLE CHURCH

The First Fifty Years (1963–2013)

Rev. Dr.

NEIL C. DAMGAARD,

ThM, DMin

WESTBOW
PRESS
A DIVISION OF THOMAS NELSON

WestBow Press books may be ordered through booksellers or by contacting:

WestBow Press
A Division of Thomas Nelson
1663 Liberty Drive
Bloomington, IN 47403
www.westbowpress.com
1-(866) 928-1240

Because of the dynamic nature of the Internet, any web addresses or links contained in this book may have changed since publication and may no longer be valid. The views expressed in this work are solely those of the author and do not necessarily reflect the views of the publisher, and the publisher hereby disclaims any responsibility for them.

Any people depicted in stock imagery provided by Thinkstock are models, and such images are being used for illustrative purposes only.
Certain stock imagery © Thinkstock.

Scripture taken from the King James Version of the Bible.

ISBN: 978-1-4497-8284-9 (sc)
ISBN: 978-1-4497-8285-6 (e)
ISBN: 978-1-4497-8286-3 (hc)

Library of Congress Control Number: 2013901587

Printed in the United States of America

WestBow Press rev. date: 2/7/2013

Acknowledgments

It is no glib or casual thing to acknowledge the living God as the source of inspiration and giver of graces by which to write a book. It is only because of the true experience of the grace of the gospel of salvation that I undertake to survey the history of one of His churches. I am thankful to Him for all my hope and every bit of energy with which He has invested me to be part of the great movement of Christianity. As it has been my privilege to minister in South Coast, Massachusetts, for the past thirty years, I wish to acknowledge the membership of the Dartmouth Bible Church for blessing me with that opportunity. I am deeply grateful to the officers and friends I have in this church who have supported me, worked alongside me, prayed for guidance, and waited for His leading so many times. I have attempted this writing because I felt like I *could* do it and because, being the church's pastor for a long time, I felt like I *should* do it. I love this church and appreciate the wonderful ways the Lord has used it in the old town of Dartmouth and beyond since 1963.

A few individuals have contributed to the effort of this history. Lisa Chan provided an early editorial review. Brendan Gahan checked my attitude and my balance on several key and tricky episodes about which I wanted to write. William Hallett Jr., who was there in the beginning of the church, gave enthusiastic support and related many good memories. Kathleen Marginson provided a late-run review and editorial commentary. Janine Soldevilla performed the data review to produce the first three appendices.

I can never thank my wife, Renée, enough for her faithful partnering with me through not only our years at Dartmouth Bible Church but through all the years before as well. I could not have engaged any ministry at all without her good humor, steady support, and candid perspective.

I began to write this history in May of 2011, and I enjoyed the eighteen months of research, writing, and rewriting. It has been a highlight of my life to undertake this project. If I have reported anything inaccurately or with imbalance, the responsibility is my own.

Neil C. Damgaard
December 2012
Dartmouth, Massachusetts

DEDICATION:
To my wife Renée and our two lovely daughters,
Jocelyn and Susanna who have each been so much
and such a pleasant part of this calling

CONTENTS

INTRODUCTION

If I could conduct a reliable poll among Christians and church attenders across the land, I imagine that almost all of them would say that they wished their own little church would last forever. Perhaps if they projected the duration of their own church, they would even predict it. However, most churches do not last beyond a few decades.[1] Some churches do endure for centuries, but most sink into decline at some point and eventually close their doors. The candle of the Bride of Christ is passed from place to place.

On the other hand, every church begins in a season of excitement and envisions meeting the spiritual needs of a new and distinct group of Christians. When they organize into a new congregation, with much prayer and a careful inventory of the assets available with which to start a church, the church is planted. It is, however, a part of God's plan that most Christians will still live metaphorically as nomads; no one place holds them long. Close to their hearts are the words of the writer of the epistle to the Hebrews: "For here we have no continuing city, but we seek one to come" (Heb. 13:14, KJV). Many churches start humbly, enjoy a time of spiritual vitality and good ministry of the Word of God, and then quietly (or not so quietly) pass away.

---

[1] According to the Barna Research Group, in research published in 2003, 60 percent of Protestant churches have one hundred or fewer adults attending on a typical weekend, while slightly less than 2 percent have one thousand or more adults. http://www.barna.org/barna-update/article/5-barna-update/126-small-churches-struggle-to-grow-because-of-the-people-they-attract. Site accessed Oct. 8, 2012.

The evangelical Protestant church history of Southeastern Massachusetts extends back to the days when the Plymouth Pilgrims began to move out from the original colony—only twenty-five miles northeast from present-day Dartmouth. John Cooke was on the *Mayflower* when it arrived in Massachusetts in November of 1620. He had been baptized at Leyden, Holland, somewhere between January and March 1607/8, and so was about thirteen years old when he arrived at Plymouth with his father, Francis Cooke.

John married Sarah Warren, daughter of *Mayflower* and *Ann* Pilgrims Richard and Elizabeth Warren, in Plymouth on March 28, 1634. He had grown up with Sarah, their families being neighbors in the new colony. John and Sarah had five daughters. John became a deacon of the Plymouth Church in the 1630s, but he was exiled from the church around 1657. Allowed to be an agent of the colony in the territory of Dartmouth, Cooke became a Baptist, which was a very new designation of independent Protestants.

He survived King Philip's War (1675–1676), though his home was burned during that sad conflict. Cooke was one of the first Baptist preachers in America, and in about 1680, he established a Baptist church in Adamsville, Rhode Island, near to present-day Tiverton. Cooke died on November 23, 1695, and was buried in what is now Fairhaven. He was the last surviving male *Mayflower* Pilgrim, having lived through the entire life of the Plymouth colony. His wife, Sarah, survived him by one year.

Cooke's Adamsville church was the beginning of a local Baptist society that has included members of many area families since its founding, some of whom eventually became part of the well-known Old Stone Church in Tiverton, built in 1841. A number of colonial churches in the Baptist tradition grew in the wider region of Bristol County but very few in the town of Dartmouth itself. In fact, when the Dartmouth Baptist Fellowship began in 1963 (then the Dartmouth Baptist Church and now the Dartmouth Bible Church), it was one of only two or three Baptist churches in the 350–year history of Dartmouth. Indeed, in doctrine, polity, and attitude, it was strikingly similar to the nation's first Baptist church, the First Baptist Church of Providence, Rhode Island, "gathered" in 1638 by Roger Williams.

Another early Massachusetts evangelical pastor who was not unfriendly to Baptist principles was Daniel Hix (1755–1838), known locally as Elder Daniel Hix. He founded the First Christian Church of Hixville in Dartmouth, Massachusetts, in 1780 when he was twenty-five years old. This church was part of the distinct movement known in southern New England as "the Christian Church," not to be confused with later and larger movements of the same name in other parts of the country. Several mission churches in Fall River, Fairhaven, Westport, Berkley, New Bedford, and Mattapoisett were founded as a result of Elder Hix's initial church plant. Hix possessed a serious discipline in his spiritual life, an evangelistic fervor, and an evangelical doctrine.

I write this history of the Dartmouth Bible Church with a sharp sense of connection with the evangelical pastors who precede me in Dartmouth and in the region. I have a great interest in the Protestant church history of this area—one of the first two English colonies in America. I feel a strong kinship with my counterparts of earlier times for both the struggles and the joys of ministry on this soil, which is so rich with American history.

In 1962, the church scene in Southeastern Massachusetts included very few churches of an evangelical doctrine and style of ministry. There were perhaps a dozen or fewer churches that were evangelical in their theology, and those spanned the widest definition of evangelical. As I write today, fifty years later, there are no less than one hundred evangelical churches in the same region in an area that is still predominantly Roman Catholic or secular-humanist in its makeup. In my thirty years here, I have watched a number of what I call "flagship" churches for our movement go into decline and other churches rise to prominence and become new "flagships." I also observe that evangelical churches usually begin with little felt need for approval from denominational hierarchies or applications for strategic brokering by "higher ups" and they rarely seek institutional financial backing before they can begin ministry. They usually just start.

It was coincidentally during the years of my ministry in Dartmouth that evangelicalism itself as a *national* movement began to recover the public notice it held before 1920. When the Dartmouth Bible Church was in its beginnings, local evangelical Protestant churches were perceived by the general public to be the fringy, distant cousins of the more established mainstream of Protestant churches. Further, as John Hannah writes,

> The terms evangelical, conservative, and fundamentalist were generally synonymous terms until the 1950s…In the years after the denominational strife of the 1920s, a coalition of conservatives/orthodox/fundamentalists emerged that sought to throw off certain negative features of the movement's past and create a new direction for the evangelical enterprise in America…This movement fractured the fragile ties that bound the older evangelical/fundamentalist movement together. As a result, a segment of the movement became a distinct entity and used the term fundamentalist exclusively, while others found it increasingly unpleasant because of its perceived identification with cultural obscurantism, intolerance, and extreme separatism.[2]

Amidst these movements, the evangelical movement in the 1960s within Protestantism began to grow again. Another writer stated, "Social groups can gain power in a variety of ways—by

---

[2] Hannah, John D. *An Uncommon Union: Dallas Theological Seminary and American Evangelicalism* (Zondervan, 2009, Kindle Locations 925-928).

voting a candidate into the Oval Office, by assuming leadership of powerful corporations, or by shaping mainstream media. Evangelicals have done them all since the late 1970s, and the change has been extraordinary."[3]

In South Coast, Massachusetts, trends in general and an evangelical presence in particular move more slowly. However, a growing network of like-minded churches has begun to draw notice here too, though they vary by denomination and to some extent in some of the specifics of theology. Because of this, I was attracted to the possibilities of contributing to the growth of a respected church with an evangelical worldview that is so near to Plymouth, the place of the nation's beginnings. At Dartmouth Bible Church, we focus on individual discipleship, nurturing healthy families, being a blessing to the town of Dartmouth and its university, and participating in meaningful ways with the larger, worldwide body of Christ. It has been my hope that DBC and its sister churches and ministries will continue to grow in vitality and make a good impact for the gospel of Jesus Christ, as was the vision of the founding families and church members in 1963. This book is also a personal history along with being a history of one church. There is a lot of me in this book, with lessons I have learned and convictions I have formed. It is secondarily a work of personal ecclesiology (the area in which I wrote my Master's thesis at Dallas Seminary.) I suppose I studied the theories of polity in seminary and then have explored those theories in practice for the next three decades.

In the context of the times and the larger spiritual picture of what God is doing, this book seeks to outline how one small church began and grew to what it is today. All of the credit for any progress made goes to the Lord Himself, with gratitude for all who faithfully participated in His program, sought His will, and served the spread of the gospel.

---

[3] Lindsay, D. Michael, *Faith in the Halls of Power: How Evangelicals Joined the American Elite,* (Oxford, UK: Oxford University Press, 2007), 2.

Chapter 1

BEGINNINGS

For ye are not come unto the mount that
might be touched... (Heb. 12:18a)

Reverend Chaloner Durfee served as pastor of the First Christian Church of Hixville from 1950 until 1963, during which time the church's membership doubled. Rev. Durfee was a 1942 graduate of B.M.C. Durfee High School in Fall River, Massachusetts. He was a member of the well-known B.M.C. (Chaloner) Durfee family of that city. During World War II, Chaloner served with a US Navy combat unit involved with naval ordinance. He married Ruth E. Dearden of Fall River in 1943 and shipped out shortly after. Ruth remembers that Chaloner began Guam for Christ, a discipleship ministry for fellow servicemen, while he was on that island and while there were still enemy soldiers holding out. After the war, Durfee attended Providence-Barrington Bible College, where he received a bachelor of arts degree in 1951 and a bachelor of theology degree in 1954. He then attended Bridgewater State College and received his master's degree in 1962. At that time, it was an unusual achievement for an evangelical pastor in Southeastern Massachusetts to hold an advanced degree.

As its pastor, Rev. Durfee was ordained by the First Christian Church of Hixville in 1955, becoming the first person to be ordained by this church in more than one hundred years. He was ordained on the occasion of the 175th anniversary of the First Christian Church of Hixville.

Reverend Chaloner Durfee

During his pastorate of First Christian Church of Hixville, Rev. Durfee was also a teacher in the Fairhaven public schools and served as president of the Fairhaven Teachers' Association. He also ministered as a board member of Youth for Christ of Fall River, a local branch of the well-known national ministry of the same name. However, in 1960, financial and other difficult conditions in the Hixville church precipitated his resignation as pastor. As so often has happened in old New England churches, when the gospel begins to be preached, some longstanding members become uncomfortable with a fresh evangelical presentation.

At this time, Rev. Durfee determined that since Dartmouth had no Baptist church, nor had one ever existed so far as he was aware, the opportunity now had presented itself to plant a Baptist church. He wished to do so close to the new proposed campus for a major university. The Southeastern Massachusetts Technical Institute of New Bedford (which would subsequently become the Southeastern Massachusetts University and later the University of Massachusetts at Dartmouth) was said to be planning a brand-new campus. That new campus would be established on land owned in part by Mr. Paul Schofield that was located on Old Westport Road, the colonial-era stage line between New Bedford and Fall River.[4] (Schofield was a cousin of Robert Schofield, a DBC member many years later.) It is not surprising that Durfee, a public educator who also possessed an evangelistic heart, would envision such an opportunity. In April of 1963, Durfee and his wife, Ruth, began a new informal fellowship in their home on Collins Corner Road, with an organizational meeting held on May 19. The first formal service was held on May 26, with twenty-four people attending. Hymnbooks were borrowed from the South Christian Church of All Nations in Freetown (an old congregation which ended its ministry in 2001). Here is the first document for the new church:

April 1963

Rev. Chaloner Durfee resings from the First Christian Church of Mixville. A meeting was called for all interested persons. The meeting was at the Pastors home. plands were being made that night to start having fellowship meetings , soon we were holding meetings in the Pastor's home Collins corner Rd. We borrowed hymn books from The South Christian Church of All Nations Freetown Mass. First Sunday there was 25 in attance. As time passed by arrangements were made to rent the V.F.W. Hall on Cross Rd. Dart. And are progessing very well, are in the process of buying land.

Order of First meeting:

Voted to fill offices:
Treasury for church Mrs. Kallet was voted to fill offices.
Board of Deacons Mr. Jorden,Mr. Kellett,Mr. Perlee.
Flower committee, Mrs. Amy Carter,Mrs. Reynolds , Mrs. Dora Roberts.

---

[4] An eighteenth-century inn still stands on that road, about a half-mile west of the present campus.

REV. Durfee was to make arrangements to meet with the head of the Baptist
Committee, to meet and talk with them to see if we would want to join the
Conference, or to stay independent.

Incharge of property (such as hymn books etc.)

Mrs . Amy Carter, Miss Anne Marie Jones. Mrs. Reis .

All interated members to meet and go over By- Laws

Salary It was agreed to pay the pastor $10.00 (Rev. Chalonor Durfee) a week,
Sunday school Treasury Mrs. Dora Roberts.

The following names;
Mrs. Amy Carter, Mrs. Lois Mc/ Cartney, Mrs. Alberta Reynolds, Mr. Clyde
                                                                Reynolds.

Mrs. Maude Parlee , Mr. Fred Parlee, Mrs. Elenor Reis, John Jones.
Barbara Reynolds, (Haskell) Charles Haskell.

asked to have their names removed from the Hixville Christian Church
membership list in order that they might unite with the Dartmouth Baptist
Fellowship.

This and all documents pictured are used by permission.

A number of Hixville church members desired to become part of
the new church plant and requested letters of dismissal from the First
Christian Church of Hixville (a protocol rarely practiced today.)
These included Amy Carter, Lois McCartney, Clyde and Alberta
Reynolds, Fred and Maude Parlee, Eleanor Reis, John Jones, and
Charles and Barbara Reynolds Haskell. A constitution and by-laws
document was drawn up for the new Dartmouth Baptist Fellowship,
based in part on that of the new Evangelical Baptist Church in South
Yarmouth, which was affiliated with the Baptist General Conference.
The original articles for the Dartmouth Baptist Fellowship included
a twelve-point affirmation of faith (which is always important and
never assumed with evangelical churches), a purpose statement, and
a church covenant, as well as various provisions for membership,
officers, services, meetings, and elections. It also included a protocol
for the role of pastor and provisions for the various committees. The
article for purpose and duty read,

The purpose of this organization shall be to maintain the public worship of God in accordance with the historic Baptist principles of fidelity to Christ and to His Word, and to further the propagation of the Gospel of Christ at home and abroad, The duty of this organization is to study, preach, and obey the Bible, the Word of God, and to administer the ordinances of the New Testament as taught by Jesus Christ.[5]

A financial statement from June 30, 1963, indicates that the new church had received $114.57 in donations to date.

The Process that Became Dartmouth Baptist Church

The new church was formed as the Dartmouth Baptist Fellowship but quickly was renamed to Dartmouth Baptist Church on December 8, 1963, with an original organizational document notarized by Percy F. Churbuck, a notary public. There were sixteen charter members, including Rev. Chaloner Durfee, Ruth Durfee, William Hallett, Sr., Dorothy Hallett, Fred Parlee, Maude Parlee, Amy Carter, Eleanor Reis, Sylvester Jordan, Thelma Jordan, Fred Valley, Margaret Valley, Paul Reed, Barbara Reed, Lloyd Taylor, and Dora Roberts. People under twenty-one years old included Ann Allen, George Brun, Brian Durfee, David Durfee, Bruce Durfee, William Hallett Jr., and James Hallett. An article from the New Bedford *Standard Times* of December 21, 1963, read:

> Adoption of a constitution and by-laws and election of officers are two of the steps taken by members of Dartmouth Baptist Fellowship toward establishing a

---

[5] From the original documents of the Dartmouth Baptist Fellowship, April 1963.

Baptist church in Dartmouth. Incorporation papers also have been filed with the State, and a building fund has been initiated. Members signed the charter of the new church to be known as Dartmouth Baptist Church. Guests present included Mr. and Mrs. George Marchak of Patterson, N.J. who previously held special services in the Hixville area. The Rev. Chaloner Durfee, pastor of the new organization, attended the quarterly business meeting of the New England Baptist General Conference at Elim Baptist Church in New Bedford. He gave a report of the progress of the newly-formed organization. Officers of the new Dartmouth church are Mr. Durfee, moderator; Mrs. Eleanor Reis, clerk; Mrs. Ruth Durfee, assistant clerk and historian; Mrs. Dorothy Hallett, financial secretary and treasurer. Mr. Durfee will also serve as superintendent of the Sunday School. Mrs. Amy Carter was also elected as Bible school treasurer. Deacons will be William Hallett Sr., Sylvester Jordan, Fred Valley and Fred Parlee. Deaconesses will be the wives of the deacons. Trustees will be Maude Parlee, Margaret Valley, Paul Reed, and Lloyd Taylor. The auditing committee will be Barbara Reed and Mrs. Durfee. Christian education committee will be Mrs. Carter and Rev. and Mrs. Durfee. Mrs. Reis and Mrs. Durfee, Publicity chairman, and Mrs. Jordan, chairman.

The state charter for Dartmouth Baptist Church is dated March 13, 1964. Jim Hallett, a young man at the time, remembers that the feeling was very good for the new church, and the prospects for growth were excellent.[6]

---

[6] Interview with William Hallett Jr. and James Hallett, May 11, 2012.

An Unexpected Passing

As providence would have it, one of Pastor Durfee's last sermons was the Christmas message for December 22, 1963, entitled, "Unto You, a Saviour." He would see the little church's first New Year's Eve program on December 31, where there was music, slides were displayed, and there was a fellowship hour with a buffet. The fledgling fellowship, however, was then presented with a great challenge when Pastor Durfee fell ill and suddenly passed away on January 25, 1964, at Union Hospital in Fall River, just nine months after the Dartmouth Baptist Fellowship began in his home. Chaloner Durfee was forty-two years old, and he left his wife, Ruth, and three sons, David, Brian, and Bruce.

In the wake of this unanticipated tragedy, the officers and members of the new church were faced with the difficult decision of whether to continue the new fellowship without Pastor Durfee's leadership or to disband. The Durfee and Hallett families were key in this decision, assisted by a few other fellowship members. In June of 2012, Bill Jr. and Jim Hallett both remembered that the decision to trust the Lord with continuance was courageously made largely based on Ruth Durfee's willingness to continue helping the church, even in the time of grieving the loss of her husband. The new Dartmouth Baptist Church continued, and the pursuit of a new pastor began.

Bill Jr. and Jim Hallett also fondly remember Barrington College's Dean Terrell B. Crum and the ministry he had as a speaker in DBC in these months. Crum was a well-known evangelical scholar at the time that had travelled with Donald G. Barnhouse, Frank E. Gaebelein, Harold J. Ockenga, and other notables. The Halletts also remembered that Dean Crum also brought some of his students to speak in the church.

A proposed budget for 1964–1965 follows:

May 7, 1964

```
            PROPOSED BUDGET FOR DARTMOUTH BAPTIST CHURCH FOR 1964-65
MISSIONS ——————————————————————————————— 10%

RENT ——————— $7 a week —————————————————————  $ 364.00

PASTOR'S SALARY —— $10 a week —————————————————   520.00

TRAVELING EXPENSE (mileage) Seven cents a mile —————————  ————

OFFICE SUPPLIES  ( $25-$50 ) ————————————————————   50.00

PUBLICITY——Bulk mailing permit; Mailing
                  ($30)            ($30)  —————————————   60.00

SPECIAL SPEAKERS, CAMPAIGNS, FILMS ————————————————   100.00

LEGAL SERVICES ———————————————————————————   25.00

DAILY VACATION BIBLE SCHOOL (DVBS) ————————————————   20.00

LAND AND BUILDING FUND ——————————————————————  ————
                                          TOTAL   $1139.00
```

Little else is recorded of those earliest days, except the courage and determination of that small group of Baptists who clung to their vision to successfully plant a vital ministry for the Word of God and the gospel in the town. Their town had such a long and colorful history, and it was a town where they had all grown up.

EARLY MINISTRIES, 1964–1965

In the year following Pastor Durfee's passing, the members of the church decided to rent the Veterans of Foreign Wars (VFW) Hall in Dartmouth for both morning and evening Sunday services. Morning services began there on August 11, 1964 and evening services on October 6. Bill Hallett Jr. remembers covering the bar area with a tarp before services, and his brother Jim remembers that it did not completely eliminate the odor of liquor! Special speakers in those days included David Lilly, an appointee with Unevangelized Fields Mission to British Guiana (now Guyana), and Bill Jones, a man who worked with youth gangs in southern Rhode Island.

Anne Marie and Lester Allen, Billy and Jim Hallett

After Dartmouth Baptist Church was granted its state charter, the members began searching for a suitable plot of land to purchase. Such a purchase would be a serious commitment to the future, and they decided on a one-acre lot on the corner of Morton Avenue and Delano Street. This property was surrounded by farmland. In fact, John "Sonny" Carter,[7] who lived across Morton Avenue, remembered that a small pond graced the Dartmouth Baptist Church lot. However, less than half a mile south of the property, construction had begun on the new Southern Massachusetts Technical Institute. Ground was broken for that institute of higher learning in June of 1964 on Old Westport Road directly across from its intersection with Morton Avenue, only six hundred yards south of the DBC property.

REVEREND JAMES HARDING

The pulpit was filled by many fine guest speakers in early 1964, and the members prayed for the Lord's guidance and leading

---

[7] Sonny Carter was proprietor of Carter Brothers Excavating and a nephew of Amy Carter, a charter member of DBC.

in the finding of a new pastor. James Harding[8] came as one of the guest speakers, and once the members spoke with him and received fine references, he was unanimously called as pastor on September 3, 1964.

Reverend James Harding

Pastor Harding was ordained to the gospel ministry on May 20, 1965, at the West Bridgewater Baptist Church. As the '60s unfolded, a brochure was printed by Pastor Harding advertising DBC. It was entitled "To Stop a Revolt" and illustrated the church's contrast with the new counterculture atmosphere of the 1960s (see Appendix 5). Pastor Harding resigned in November 1968, however,

---

[8] Years later I would (by coincidence) befriend Harding's father, Rev. Henry Harding, as we were both members of the Southeastern Massachusetts Evangelical Ministers' Fellowship. Henry Harding was associate pastor of a Baptist Church in Weymouth at the time and later a resident of Rumney, New Hampshire, where I fellowshipped with Henry many times in years to follow.

to go with his wife, Joan, and family to Africa with the Africa Inland Mission. After deputation and commissioning, the Hardings set sail on August 23, 1970, to assume their duties at the Rift Valley Academy in Kenya, Africa. Rev. and Mrs. Harding were warmly welcomed back to DBC in September 1983 on the occasion of the church's twentieth anniversary (my first major event as pastor of DBC), and Rev. Harding once again visited DBC for the dedication of our second building in August of 2000 (see above). His ministry was recognized for its importance in the early years as well as his and Joan's faithfulness to the gospel and to their calling as missionaries. James and Joan Harding remain good friends of DBC to this day. They are now retired and living in Longview, Texas.

PURCHASE OF LAND AT MORTON AVENUE AND DELANO STREET

It was a historical coincidence that land was purchased at the corner of Morton and Delano Streets in Dartmouth.[9] Construction of the Dartmouth Baptist Church in 1968 provided the town of Dartmouth with only its second Baptist church building in a history dating back to the mid-1600s. While Chaloner Durfee believed Dartmouth Baptist Church would be the first Baptist church in the town's history, it is, in fact, the second. An earlier Baptist church,

---

[9] The tract of land in which the intersection lies is found within the old Dartmouth zoning as "Morton Park," a name that tracks back very far in Dartmouth history. Morton and Delano were two original Plymouth surnames from the first colony. Thomas Morton was a *Fortune* "saint" (1621) with connections in Dartmouth through his brother, George (an *Anne* "saint", 1623, but died in 1624), and his wife Juliana, who in 1627 married *Anne* "stranger" Menassah Kempton and "removed to Dartmouth" in about 1652. Phillipe De La Noye (Delano) was born to French Protestant parents and was the progenitor of an important name in the Dartmouth and Fairhaven areas. He was also a *Fortune* "saint" and lived in Duxbury and then Bridgewater. (*Saints and Strangers* by George F. Willison, 1945, Parnassus Imprints.)

South Dartmouth Baptist Church,[10] was once apparently located on Bakerville Road.

The significance is not diminished, though, as the town's records indicate that Dartmouth Baptist Church is the first Baptist church seen in the town at least since the mid-1800s, and indeed, what is now Bristol County can be argued to have seen the first of the nation's Baptist churches *at all*. Roger Williams, founder of the first Baptist church in the nation in Providence, Rhode Island, spent time in what is now Swansea and Rehoboth, Massachusetts.

The members of Dartmouth Baptist Church purchased a one-acre lot for $1,200 from Mr. John H. Brown. Mr. Brown stated that he would rather the land be used for a new church than for more homes. The note was paid off on September 7, 1965, in just one year.

---

[10] Hurd, D. Hamilton, *History of Bristol County Massachusetts.* (Philadelphia, PA: J.W. Lewis, 1883), 204

Only two years after its beginning in the Durfees' living room, the new Dartmouth Baptist Church owned the land on which it now stands. A number of original church members lived in the immediate neighborhood of the purchased lot. The Valleys lived on the corner of Morton and Delano, the Jordans across the street on Delano, Amy Carter lived in the fourth house on Delano, and the Halletts lived down the street on Cross Road. Dorothy Hallett had been born in a nearby house in 1921.

AFFILIATION

Dartmouth Baptist Church became affiliated with the Baptist General Conference of New England on May 13, 1965, and as such became an official sister church of the only other BGC church in the area—Elim Baptist Church of New Bedford. This was DBC's second indirect tie to the past—first with DBC charter members coming out of the very old Hixville Church and then official fellowship with Elim Baptist Church (which later would send members in the 1991 merger). Affiliation with the BGC lasted until December 1981 but was then reestablished in 1994.[11]

CONSTRUCTION OF 52 MORTON AVENUE

A building committee was established on November 8, 1965, and construction began with ground-breaking on October 29, 1967, with the first spade turned over by charter member Maude Parlee. The building was completed in the spring of 1968, and the first service in the new building was held on June 2, 1968. According to Bill Hallett, Jr., "After the erection of the framework and exterior of the building, most of the interior and finish work

---

[11] I have appreciated the Conference, though I had never before been part of a denomination, and I was glad to subsequently serve as a Northeast Baptist Conference trustee, the New England district of the BGC, for six years, from 2000 to 2006.

was provided by the men and women of the church itself." The architect was a Mr. Ken Perry, who had provided architectural services for other BGC ministries, and the contractor was a Mr. Pardini from Seekonk.

Maude Parlee and Selectmen and Jim Harding in hat

William Hallett Sr. wrote and read this prayer at the building's dedication in June of 1968:

> Our heavenly Father, we thank Thee today for the privilege and joy of being together in Thy house and Thy presence to offer our prayer and to sing praises to Thee and to our risen Savior, Jesus Christ.
>
> We thank Thee again, Lord, for Thy answers to our many prayers. We thank Thee for our church charter. May we bring honor and glory to Thy name.
>
> We pray for those who are sick among us and are unable to be with us. Be close to them in their hour of need, and touch them with healing and mercy ...

EARLY CONFERENCES

It has been a part of evangelical church tradition since the turn of the twentieth century to hold Bible conferences, mission conferences, Christian education, and Christian life conferences from time to time. Dartmouth Baptist Church embraced this tradition (and continues it today). In the early years, the church family enjoyed various conferences provided by Bible teachers from the Providence Bible Institute, which later became Barrington College and subsequently merged with Gordon College of Wenham, Massachusetts. Occasionally missionaries were invited to speak and share their work on the mission field. One presentation by Dr. James Knorr in 1974 included a slide presentation of the "Lands of the Travels of St. Paul." Also in that year Rev. David Rivers of Gospel Communications, Inc., shared a dramatic characterization of the Roman centurion at the cross. Dr. Donald Sunukjian from Dallas Theological Seminary also took the dramatic approach much later as a guest speaker in 1986 when he acted out the book of Esther.

Chapter 2

SHORT PASTORATES, THEN A LONG ONE

Remember them which have rule over you. who have
spoken unto you the word of God ... (Heb. 13:7a)

REVEREND RAY LEAVITT

Ray Leavitt, who was the bookstore manager at Barrington
College, began as part-time interim pastor of Dartmouth
Baptist Church in late 1970. His pastoral ministry at DBC lasted
until 1973. Rev. Leavitt had been one of the guest speakers after the
Hardings departed for Africa. On November 29, 1970, he was called
as interim pastor.

Even though Rev. Leavitt did not feel
led to become the permanent pastor of
DBC, he had a good ministry among the
people of the church. Under his gentle
guidance, there was a renewing of faith
and courage, and several new families
joined DBC. During this time, four sisters
began attending, Elizabeth Thurman,

Janice McFadden, Rosemary Carlisle (later Alves), and Kathie Carlisle (later Marginson). Kathie remembers one evangelistic outreach in 1972 during which a number of young people were brought in from out of the region through an evangelistic organization and hosted by church families. The young people went door to door sharing the gospel with families in the neighborhood. A farewell party was held by the church for the Leavitt family on January 28, 1973. In 1980, Pastor Leavitt returned to perform the wedding of Kathie Carlisle to Thomas Marginson at Elim Baptist Church in New Bedford. The Marginsons remain valued and honored members of DBC to this day.

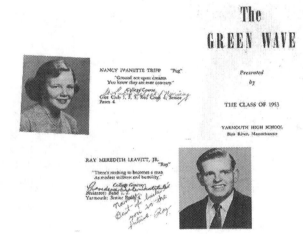

Through an Internet search, I was able to locate Ray and Betty Leavitt in October 2012. The Leavitts now live in Hendersonville, North Carolina, and I was able to interview them both via telephone.[12] They have followed Dartmouth Bible Church in recent years, they said, by following the church's website. Rev. Leavitt, now seventy-seven years old, said that he fondly remembers his time at DBC (forty years ago) as, among all his ministries, "the

---

[12] Telephone interview with Ray and Elizabeth Leavitt, October 31, 2012.

one in which I did the least and the Lord did the most." He shared that he agreed to come to DBC as an interim pastor, retaining his post as bookstore manager at Barrington College, on the condition that the church would hold no business meetings for one year and would concentrate on worship, Bible study, prayer, and outreach—a condition to which the church agreed. There was a core of only a half-dozen or so active leaders in the church. As a postscript, Ray also shared that he had graduated from high school in 1953 alongside (the late) longtime DBC member Nancy Tripp Graham, of whom he had fond memories. Nancy did not begin to attend DBC until the ministry of Mel Longtin.

REVEREND DR. DON ANDERSON

Reverend Dr. Don Anderson was Dartmouth Baptist Church's fourth pastor, serving from 1973 until 1975. I was privileged to meet with him on December 7, 2011. Dr. Anderson, now sixty-four years old, is currently the Executive Minister of the Rhode Island State Council of Churches in Providence. He reminisced, "Ray Leavitt preached his last sermon on one Sunday, and I preached my first the next Sunday." This seamless transition is unique in DBC's history.

Don desired to serve DBC part-time while beginning his seminary studies at a nearby seminary, either Gordon Conwell Theological Seminary or Andover-Newton in Boston. He decided on Andover-Newton. He was originally from Cranston, Rhode Island, and graduated with his bachelor's degree from Barrington College in 1970. He also worked in the Barrington College bookstore and brought a business background to his ministry. Dr. Anderson had hoped that half of his salary could be funded by the Baptist General Conference mission-church support fund and half from the budget of Dartmouth Baptist Church. The church's entire annual budget in Anderson's years ranged from about $6,000 to $10,000. However, the church had never received any instruction on protocols for this, and so during his ministry he was not paid a salary by the church and he ministered uncompensated for the most part by the church itself. Don's wife at that time was Gerrie Anderson, who was a teacher at the Christian School in Fall River. She brought much to the church in the area of Christian education.

Dr. Anderson describes his gifts as being primarily in the areas of preaching and teaching. He now notes that he has no musical ability, and at the time of his ministry, he had no foresight for the musical needs of the church. He reflects that, in general, a church will hire its next pastor (consciously or unconsciously) with strengths not held by the previous pastor. This gives some explanation to the church's choice of his successor. Don remembers the importance during those years of charter members Bill Hallett Sr. and Dorothy Hallett, who had a "wonderful and great spirit." He also remembers, interestingly, that there were no weddings or funerals during his two-year ministry. Fred and Maude Parlee, also charter members, were still in the church though home-bound because of poor health. It was during this time that cassette recording was becoming popular, and the church purchased a cassette recorder so the Parlees could be given a tape of each week's service. Don laughs about his own lack of musical ability with the story of a day when he went to visit the Parlees, and they insisted that he listen to his own singing on the tape, in its entirety. When he objected, they said, "No, pastor, we had to listen to the whole tape—now you do too!"

Under Dr. Anderson's ministry, the large Martin family was brought into the church.

Reverend Don Anderson

In an August 2011 interview, Mike Martin remembers Pastor Don as an "arm around you" and an "encourager" kind of pastor. He was a peaceful fellow, with a Plymouth Brethren background. Martin said Pastor Don brought a "good number of people into DBC," including some who had been associated with the Christian School of Fall River. He described Anderson as a fellow who brought individuals into the church, whereas his successor, Pastor Mel Longtin, was a pastor who brought *ideas* into the church (as well as being an excellent mentor). Anderson himself relates that David Martin had come to faith through the radio ministry (*Songtime*) of John DeBrine and subsequently brought his brothers George and Michael and their families into the church. He remembered that they were all baptized in Elim Baptist Church's baptistery and were apprehensive about whether the water was old in the baptistery and thereby unsanitary, as they had been warned in their Catholic upbringing. Reassured by Anderson that the Elim water would be fresh, they were joyfully baptized there! Don Anderson remembers at least three DBC baptism services during his ministry hosted by Elim, since Dartmouth Bible Church did not yet possess a baptistery. Anderson also remembered one other church-life detail: during at least two summers there was a joint Elim-Dartmouth softball team that competed in an area church softball league.

Don began a Bible study in David and Evie Martin's home that grew eventually to five weekly Bible studies, mostly evangelistic. One of the Bible studies, Don remembers, attracted a group of single mothers who wanted to study God's Word together.

During these days, there was always a small group of students from nearby Southeastern Massachusetts University attending, perhaps five students at any given time. Don relates that he was officially named as the Protestant chaplain at SMU and enjoyed his brief time of ministry there. A Vacation Bible School was first instituted at DBC in this time also, with door-to-door invitations distributed to neighborhood children. This first VBS saw thirty children attend and was a great affirmation to the church. Don reflects that the timing for new ministries was very ripe, and he felt privileged to be part of it. Don also remembers his friendship with Rev. Manuel Chavier Sr., who encouraged him to not "burn himself out" with church work. Rev. Chavier gave Don a sense of freedom to enjoy a day off, a Sabbath rest. Chavier's ministry at International Church of the Nazarene, a large church located in downtown New Bedford, was at its peak, and he was held in high esteem in the community until his passing in 2006. Don Anderson, then a new and inexperienced pastor in his late twenties, valued Rev. Chavier's affirmation and encouragement.

Reverend Bill Stroup

Bill Stroup was an assistant pastor in Pennsylvania and a graduate of the Practical Bible School of New York and Calvary Bible College in Kansas City (BA, 1968). Don Anderson believes that Bill's musical abilities were one reason why he was hired His wife, Mary Ellen, was also a graduate of both schools.

Stroup was working as a typesetter in Kansas when he was contacted by Dartmouth Baptist Church's pulpit committee and subsequently called as the pastor of DBC in May of 1975. He served until April 1976. Bill and Mary Ellen had two children. From DBC, Pastor Bill went into missions work with WorldVenture, formerly known as the Conservative Baptist Foreign Missionary Society, where he and his family served in the Congo from 1980 to 1998.[13]

Reverend and Mrs. William Stroup

[13] Via the "Linked In" website.

REVEREND MELVIN LONGTIN

Mel Longtin, raised in New Bedford and married to the former Susan Hall, became DBC's pastor in October 1976. Mel was ordained by Calvary Bible Church of Westport in November of that year. He had served in Calvary as a deacon, chairman of the Christian education board, Sunday school teacher, and visitation and discipleship leader, and he had preached at Dartmouth Baptist Church as a guest speaker before being called as an interim pastor. Mel was a graduate of New Bedford Vocational High School and earned a B.S. in Bible at Philadelphia College of the Bible. DBC grew under Pastor Mel's ministry, and Mel and Susan ministered in DBC until March 1980, when they relocated to Florida, where they still reside today.

Reverend and Mrs. Mel Longtin

Mel was also described by Mike Martin as a "trainer" who was interested in organization and that he worked often with the leaders of the church in discipling and teaching them. He envisioned *how* the church could really function better with a deeper sense of family and church body life. He was enthusiastic about cell groups. He and Susan had led one before they came to DBC. The term *cell group* has been replaced in recent years by the term *small group*, which remains a very popular platform for ministry and fellowship. Cell groups are semi-permanent fellowships of Christians that often meet in homes instead of at a church. They focus on Bible study, prayer, and forming satisfying relationships. Kathie Marginson also remembers one significant Old Testament survey course taught by Mel that really showcased his gift of teaching. Mel provided study notes and took a more academic approach than the church had seen to that point.

Mel and Susan Longtin today

When I met with her in August 2011, Susan Longtin described her husband as having a structured life and ministry while at DBC.

From their involvement with the Overseas Christian Servicemen's Center in Newport, Rhode Island, they brought several people into DBC, including Jack and Priscilla Wright, Ed and Mary Sylvia, and Tom and Pat DeCosta.

Susan also remembers several renovation projects, including finishing the old building's ground level, adding an exterior French drain around the building, and re-shingling the outside of the building. There was also a restart of Vacation Bible School in 1977 and the use of Bible study materials by well-known Texas preacher "Colonel" R. B. Thieme, who took a very academic and also militaristic approach to study. The church possessed a strong hunger for the study of the Word of God, yet skilled and educated Bible teachers were seldom available. For a few years during the early 1980s, DBC offered Bible classes from the National Institute of Biblical Studies (NIBS). These classes were on video cassette, which was a new technology at the time. The church purchased the videos and a VHS player and provided weekly Bible instruction from some excellent, nationally known teachers, such as Stuart Briscoe and J. I. Packer. This enabled the church members and attendees access to good Bible teaching, which carried into the time when there would be no pastor.[14]

Pastor Mel also brought in the first use of "praise choruses" and led them himself on Sunday mornings, accompanied by others on guitars. He also happily participated in Baptist General Conference activities, which Susan says he enjoyed. She remembers that the main leaders of the church during their years in DBC were Mike Martin, Tom DeCosta, and Bill Hallett Sr. A high-water mark in attendance for the early years was noted for April 6, 1980, with 115 people attending the worship service. On January 19, 1977, charter member Maude Parlee designated Dartmouth Baptist Church the beneficiary of a portion of her estate (several thousand dollars)

---

[14] NIBS, as a national ministry, became defunct around 1987.

with the establishment of the Parlee Fund in her last will and testament. This fund was expended by 1990 but was of great help for upkeep and maintenance during lean times. Happily, Mel and Susan renewed their fellowship at DBC, beginning in 2005, while visiting from Florida in the summers. He continues to possess a keen theological mind and a great capacity for reading, processing biblical subjects, and dialoging about them as an encouragement to believers.

In 1980, the first imagining of a new building began. Even with a small congregation, space needs were becoming critical in the original building. Families were having more children, and church activities were increasing as the "body life" concepts were explored. A "Building Research Committee" convened on February 12, 1980, including Victor Gonsalves, Craig Mechler, and Susan Longtin. A conviction of the committee, under Pastor Longtin's advice, was to consider the impact of a new facility on the church's potential ministry in the community. This process would become dormant until 1989, however, but it is worthy of note that first conceptions of expansion date to this time (first sketch below). The vision for a church that would be a blessing to the wider community was something I also felt would be honoring to the Lord.

Plymouth Brethren Leanings

In the early 1980s, after the departure of Pastor Longtin, some leaders in DBC had become enamored with certain Plymouth Brethren principles:[15] the "open" meeting approach in worship, no paid clergy,

---

[15] The Plymouth Brethren began in Dublin, Ireland, around 1827 and spread to the rest of Great Britain. It is a conservative and evangelical Christian movement characterized by a lack of official clergy, the weekly celebration of the Lord's Supper, and other practices. "Brethren" churches are fiercely independent and generally fall into two categories: "open" brethren, and "exclusive" brethren.

and church government by elder rule. During this time, Michael Martin was one of the main church leaders, capably providing much of the preaching and giving a sense of somebody being in charge. He served as an elder from 1983 until 1985. Although he abruptly departed the church in September 1985, Michael renewed contact with some of his former DBC friends in 2009 and shared his testimony of God's grace and how God had worked in his life in recent years.

BECOMING A BIBLE CHURCH

During 1980, after the departure of Mel Longtin, the leaders of the church became increasingly disaffected with their affiliation with the Baptist General Conference. They were not feeling much a part of the BGC or seeing much value in affiliation. These young leaders identified more closely with some of the better-known contemporary and nondenominational Bible teachers such as Gene Getz, John MacArthur, and Ray Stedman—respected pastors and teachers from the "Bible Church" movement. Therefore, the leaders, with no permanent pastor in their employ, decided to seek dissolution with the Baptist General Conference.

A letter of detachment was sent to the Conference on December 18, 1981. The church was informed by the then District Executive Minister, Wes Lindbloom, in a letter dated January 11, 1982, that since the church was withdrawing from affiliation with the conference, they would be expected to repay money given to them by the BGC to help with the construction of the church building. The amount was listed as $8,203.72. The logic as expressed in this letter was that the BGC needed to be a good steward of its resources and recover any seed-money invested. Dartmouth Baptist Church then announced the name change to Dartmouth Bible Church in *The Standard-Times* on April 30, 1982, having complied with the requirements for a corporation name change by the secretary of the Commonwealth of Massachusetts, who was petitioned to register the name change. The outstanding balance was paid back to the Conference in full by 1984.

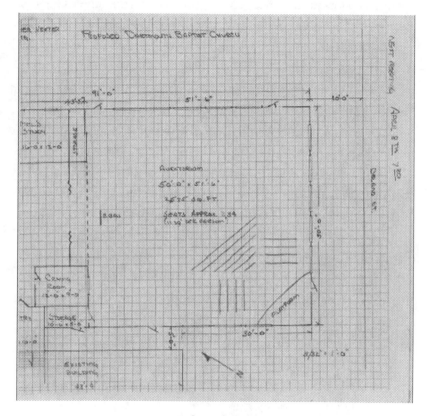

A first sketch

Tom and Pat DeCosta began attending DBC under the ministry of Pastor Mel Longtin at about the same time that Mel began his ministry in 1976. The DeCostas worshipped and ministered in DBC until January 1983. An interview with Tom in January 2012 provided an interesting picture of how things in DBC were in those years from his perspective. He deeply regrets now that the older people of the church were displaced by the younger and more energetic people, who were predominantly new Christians. In fact, Tom feels plainly that the older people were decidedly, if not intentionally, maneuvered out of the church by the younger people. Leadership decisions had become almost exclusively the domain of the new, younger leaders. The feel of worship was more contemporized, further alienating the more traditionally minded people. Almost none of the earlier leaders remained in DBC, and a whole new church family was growing up at 52 Morton Avenue.

More happily, Tom DeCosta remembers that soon after Pastor Mel's departure from DBC, Ron and Kathy Davis began attending, and though they only lived in the area for a short while, they provided a much-needed sense of stability for the church. Ron Davis was also remembered by Mike Martin for being a great blessing and bringing "a contribution of stability that was very much needed." The Davis's relocated to Scottsboro, Alabama, prior to 1982. Tom also mentioned J. P. Smith, who was a Sunday school teacher and deacon "of the old school"; Jack Wright of a more Plymouth Brethren leaning; Bob Whitlow as a young believer who "really knew how to love"; and Victor Gonsalves, whom Tom remembers exploring the eldership for a short time when that term was still very new for DBC. He also says the clear leaders were Pastor Mel, Michael Martin, Donald Laprade, and himself. A deliberate effort was underway to remake DBC along more literally biblical lines, including polity, authenticity in worship, and closer groups for fellowship.

The DeCostas, however, then relocated for a time to Pittsfield, Massachusetts, as members of the staff of Lakeside Camp, a year-round Christian camp and retreat center operated by the Northeast Baptist Conference. During their time at Lakeside, the DeCostas became acquainted with Gary Stephens, who would much later become a DBC-supported missionary to Cameroon, Africa. Tom describes the years he was associated with DBC as "not fun" years but a time when he and Pat never lost their "joy of the Lord."

He also remembers another Bible teacher, Dr. S. Lewis Johnson, whom he met at a conference in Attleboro. He was impressed with Dr. Johnson's presentation of the Word of God. (Coincidentally, Dr. Johnson was also at that time an influence on me while Renée and I were still in Virginia and then Texas. He later became a friend!) A summarizing memory for Tom is the affection and appreciation he had for the dedication of Pastor Mel Longtin to the Word of God.

REVEREND JOHN FERNANDEZ

After Pastor Longtin and his family moved to Florida in 1980, Reverend John Fernandez of California was hired to serve as an interim pastor for six months, from July 1981 until February 1982. Pastor Fernandez was a friend of Dartmouth Bible Church members Donald and Roberta Laprade, who had lived in California for a time. It was John's wife, Pam Fernandez, who began the "Secret Sisters" ministry program in DBC, which is still running as of 2012.

A June 2011 chat with former deacon Don Laprade was helpful, as Don remembers his years in DBC with wife Roberta and their three children from 1976 to 1984. Mel Longtin was the newly installed pastor when Don and Roberta moved to Acushnet from California. Don recalls that most of the congregation consisted of young families with many small children, that the church building did not have enough room for Sunday School classes and a nursery, and that the building had a problem with dampness in the basement. He also remembers that all the leaders were inexperienced churchmen even though they were sincere and worked hard to lead DBC as best they could and that Pastor Longtin was an excellent listener, a capable Bible teacher and thinker, and a stabilizing force during his three-and-a-half-year ministry. Don remembers the important roles David and Evie

Martin played, with "strong and confident leadership but without any feeling of intimidation." Don's dominant memory is of the difficulty of so many shepherding issues, for which none or few of the leaders were equipped or experienced to handle. Don observes, "It occurred to me after a while, 'This is not fun.'"

OTHER EARLY 1980S LEADERS

The story of Dartmouth Bible Church is by no means only a story of its pastors. Many other dedicated Christian leaders rose to the occasion of the need for leadership and innovation at various times. Some of those from the early 1980s include the following:

- *Craig and Susan Mechler.* Craig served as a music leader and had been in Calvary Bible Church (Westport) for a while. They had left DBC before I came in 1983.
- In the early 1980s, *Jonathan and Debbie Donner* both began attending DBC after leaving Calvary Bible Church, which Debbie had attended as a child. Jon and Debbie proved to be important members in these years and more so much later, as Jon helped with music in the church, along with his younger friend, *Mark Amaral.* Both Jon and Debbie continue to bless DBC to this day with their gifts and love for the body.
- *Jack and Priscilla Wright* were close friends of Pastor Mel Longtin and later were important in the ministry of Crossroads Bible Chapel (Dartmouth). They were in DBC for less than a year, departing before I arrived. In later years, I befriended two of the Wrights' sons, each of whom occasionally attended DBC.
- *Joel Burns*, a much-respected member and a New Bedford *Standard-Times* newspaper executive, served as DBC's moderator.

- *David and Cheryl Tomasia* left DBC at the same time that we arrived. The three Tomasia families (David and Cheryl, *John and Maria,* and *Jim and Marie*) provided a contrasting presence in DBC while they were here. They were serious Christians but heard a different kind of call. Jim and Marie were in DBC for the longest amount of time.

Dartmouth Bible Church had become a small and close-knit, charmingly informal, and needy congregation by 1983. During that spring, DBC included about thirty-five adults and twenty-five children. Very hard and sincere work by the leaders and a sense of togetherness held the "family" together. Mike Martin provided most of the Sunday preaching, while the other members were heavily involved with other aspects of the ministry, such as children's programs, outreach, and building maintenance. There was a sense of ownership among the members as they worked together to perform the needed tasks. By this time, though, all the older people had left DBC and the congregation was fairly unified, if "huddled against the storm" of few assets, little money, and spiritual youth. Nevertheless, the body explored new ministries while waiting on the Lord to provide a full-time shepherd.

CANDIDATES FOR THE NEXT PASTORATE

Despite the influence of the Plymouth Brethren sympathizers, the leaders of Dartmouth Bible Church saw the need for a full-time pastor. They decided to contact Dallas Theological Seminary for possible candidates to pursue, and two men's names were provided by the seminary for the church to invite to "candidate."

- Rev. Fred McRae, a Dallas Seminary graduate, candidated at DBC in early 1982 but ultimately decided to become a missionary with Greater Europe Mission.

- Rev. Roger Litfin, brother of Dr. Duane Litfin (the seventh president of the well-known evangelical Wheaton College in Illinois), candidated at DBC in September 1982 but declined to further pursue a calling here. It was from Litfin that I first heard about DBC. I was on the stairway of the Student Center at Dallas Seminary when I overheard him talking about a little church he had visited in Massachusetts.

REVEREND NEIL DAMGAARD

In October of 1982, I was a fourth-year Master of Theology (Th.M.) student at Dallas Theological Seminary. I had been ordained by Grace Church in Roanoke, Virginia, in August of that year after a year-long process. Upon overhearing about DBC from recent pastoral candidate, Roger Litfin, I learned that he had visited DBC that September. He said that though they were a very sincere fellowship of fine believers in New England, he had not chosen to pursue a calling there.

I inquired with then-DTS Placement Director Robert Salstrom about the church. As I stood in his office, Salstrom dialed Donald Laprade of DBC on the telephone and abruptly handed the phone to me! That began a series of telephone interviews, leading to an invitation to candidate during Easter weekend of 1983. Subsequently, the members of Dartmouth Bible Church voted to extend a call to me. After much prayer and consideration, Renée and I decided that I should accept the call to be their pastor. I was thirty years old. Renée and I, and our six-month-old daughter, Jocelyn, moved to New Bedford in May 1983, immediately after graduation from Dallas Theological Seminary. We were excited at the potential for growth and ministry that we saw in this small church. My ministry began without fanfare or ceremony on Sunday, May 29, 1983. Attendance that day was around thirty adults. The church possessed about

$6,000 in cash assets, along with its mortgage and its loan debt to the Baptist General Conference.

SUMMER 1983 AND AFTER

We arrived in Dartmouth to a small group of leaders who were very sincere and intent in their faith. These included deacons Don Laprade, Mike Martin, Russell Vieira, and Bob Whitlow. There were no elders in place. Other key people in the church included Bob and Nancy Graham (the eldest in the church, in their mid-forties), Tom and Kathie Marginson, Jerry and Diane Corkum, Michael and Susan Ponte, John and Maria Tomasia, Jim and Marie Tomasia, Larry and Cheryl Carlysle, Greg and Sheila Aleman, and singles Ron Brunette and Barry and Vivian Mingola. Mr. Milton Reed, sixty-five years old and an early DBC member, returned to the church not long after we arrived. After checking me out in a thorough if informal interview one afternoon that summer, he said to me, "You'll do."

Maria Tomasia, who worked as an aide to then U.S. Congressman Gerry Studds, composed and copied the weekly bulletin each week. (She subsequently became Elections Commissioner for the City of New Bedford where she serves in that role to this day.) John and Maria Tomasia were especially kind and accommodating to us and seemed to sense that we were coming to a difficult ministry. Some other notable recollections of our early days in DBC:

- Church finances were very tight. The church was still repaying money loaned to them by the Baptist General Conference for construction of the church building. A $12,000 balance on the 1968 mortgage also remained, and the priority among the leaders was to pay off the mortgage, which was done within a short while after our arrival. My salary that first year was $18,298.

- When Renée, Jocelyn, and I arrived in Dartmouth, the church leadership secured an apartment for us. It was the second-floor apartment in a two-family "tenement" on Collins Street in New Bedford owned by friends of Don and Roberta Laprade. On the Saturday that we moved in, church people provided groceries and staple items for the pantry. Tom Marginson, a New Bedford firefighter, took me to "Service News" on Pope's Island to purchase a city map, and then he drove me around New Bedford, pointing out important buildings and places of interest. Like many in the church, Tom was born in the area and had lived here his whole life. Bob and Joan Whitlow provided a refrigerator for our apartment, and a few months later, Mike Martin hooked up his spare "Humphrey heater" so we could have heat for the winter. The church family seemed so glad that we had arrived.

- There were two missionary families listed on the budget, but support had not been sent to either for some time due to lack of funds: Dave and Evie Martin, who ran a camp ministry in Pennsylvania, and Mr. and Mrs. Walter Davenport, associated with the Overseas Christian Servicemen's Center in Newport.[16]

- Our second daughter, Susanna Jo, was born on November 10, 1984, at Charlton Memorial Hospital in nearby Fall River. By then, we had moved to a larger apartment, located in a two-family tenement on Rockdale Avenue in New Bedford. Greg and Sheila Aleman, who soon thereafter relocated to

---

[16] Coincidentally, Renée and I were longtime friends of OCSC chaplains Gordon and June Gustafson of Panama and Cadiz, Spain, for whom we had great respect. Gordon had been attending a Bible study on board the USS *Tennessee* when the attack on Pearl Harbor occurred and subsequent to the war, served with OCSC for many years. The Gustafsons prayed regularly for the Damgaards. We certainly knew of the OCSC ministry!

Virginia, were particularly kind to us during this time by providing friendship and babysitting.

- A common saying in seminary at that time for church candidates, though a bit dark, was, "Beware of who picks you up at the airport." I had heard this often and was especially alert to the potential to lose to the church leaders who had worked hard in the interim between pastors in holding the church together. Nonetheless, within two years of our coming, DBC would lose most of its male leaders, despite my best efforts to befriend and encourage them. This was a challenge that depressed and haunted me for years. The faithfulness of the remaining leaders, especially Bob Whitlow, sustained me, as did the Lord Himself, of course.

- God does provide, however! It was only for a year, but *Charlie and Marilyn Rand* came into DBC and immediately made a place for themselves. Charlie was an engineer with General Electric and was assigned to the Acushnet Company in New Bedford for a short time. The Rands began attending DBC and were a great encouragement, especially to Renée and me. They purchased a washer and dryer for us while we still lived on Collins Street in 1983, and they also befriended several other DBC families. We were so financially lean, and their goodness to us was humbling and greatly appreciated. The Rands now live in Virginia and remain friends to this day.

- On the positive side, this also was a time that the church family contributed by a special gift—enough money to pay for the closing costs for us to purchase a home on Willow Street (vintage 1879). Madeline Sinclair was instrumental in collecting gifts from individuals in the church body. We were very grateful, and our purchase of a house was taken as a signal by the church that we intended to make New Bedford our home for a while.

- It was also at that time that the Lord brought *Betty Forbes* to DBC, a recently widowed sister in Christ from Arkansas. She first visited DBC the Sunday before our daughter Susanna was born and immediately began a ministry of kindness and encouragement to the Damgaard family that lasted until she was called home to Christ in September 2000. One special memory is how Betty generously provided the money for airline tickets so we could fly to Roanoke, Virginia, and attend the funeral of Renee's father, Commander Morley English, in March 1985. She was special to all in DBC and became best of friends with Chris Ferguson. She is still missed.

Chapter 3

CONNECTIONS

And whether one member suffer, all the members
suffer with it; or one member be honoured, all the
members rejoice with it. (1st Cor. 12:26)

It is intuitive that New Testament churches and ministries need one
another. Contrary to the fiercely independent heritage of our own
region, it has seemed to me that some kind of interconnectedness
is appropriate, expedient, and honoring to the Lord. Dartmouth
Bible Church has sought and enjoyed connections with other like-
minded churches and ministries both in our area and outside. Those
contemporary connections hint at the greater connection in spirit
and doctrine between DBC *and the past* through Elim, Hixville,
Pacific Union, Mullein Hill, and other much older churches.

SISTER CHURCHES

An important part of the work of the body of Christ is to promote
and contribute to the overall unity of the body and the work of
the kingdom. Historically, Protestant churches in our area tend to
be fiercely independent and separatistic—a noble feature in some

Neil C. Damgaard

regards but sometimes indicative of an unhealthy elitism. DBC has sought to be connected within healthy parameters through most of its history. Notable connections we have made are summarized as follows.

The "Triad"

DBC, Elim Baptist Church, and the Northeast Baptist Conference together comprised what was locally known as "The Triad" in the early 1970s. It lasted for a few years and interestingly brought Rev. David Schaffer into good fellowship with DBC even in the earliest years of his ministry at Elim.

The Northeast Baptist Conference of the Baptist General Conference

The on-again, off-again, on-again relationship with the Baptist General Conference has impacted DBC only minimally over the years. DBC had originally affiliated with the BGC in its beginning and then disaffiliated in 1982. However, as the church grew, and after the merger with Elim Baptist Church, there was the idea of seeking affiliation once again. Driving the impulse to re-affiliate in 1994 was the conviction that the conference had recently developed newer priorities and a fresh missions-mindedness that seemed more compatible to our own. In recent years as well, DBC has felt an affinity to the particular BGC (now called *Converge*) missionaries we have come to support.

During the years 2000 through 2006, I served as a district trustee to the BGC. This service afforded me a closer interest and more personal contact with district growth for those years. Our district is now called *Converge Northeast* and comprises approximately eighty churches in New England. With affiliation for DBC, there is some more feeling of connection and also some sense of legitimization for the reputation of the church. Independent Protestant churches

40

sometimes struggle to establish validity in the public eye. Our connection with the BGC/*Converge* addressed to some extent the problem of identity. People often inquire, "With whom are you affiliated?" We now have an answer to that question.

ELIM BAPTIST CHURCH (1899)

Elim Baptist Church of New Bedford was founded in 1899 as the Swedish Baptist Mission church. It began as a series of meetings in homes among young Scandinavian believers in 1893 and the next year was welcomed to use the parlor of the First Baptist Church of New Bedford. The church's name was taken from Exodus 15:27, "then they came to Elim where there were twelve springs of water and seventy date palms, and they camped there beside the waters."

Elim's first pastor, in 1895, was Rev. A. F. Borgendahl. The church has an interesting past and is closely linked to the rich history of the City of New Bedford. The Elim building on Middle Street was purchased in May 1896 for $3,200 and was originally the Second Baptist Church. Other details include the raising of money to bring water service to the Middle Street church building, a three-day bazaar by the "Ladies Mission Circle," the donation of a new organ by a Mrs. Swaim (mother of First Baptist's pastor), and the installation of a baptistery in 1900. The house that was later attached to the church building, known as the Martin Pierce House,[17] was purchased in 1955, renovated for use by Elim, and dedicated in September 1956.

Elim's whole history was completely defined in the Baptist tradition, and many people were ministered to and served within this fine church body through all of its nine decades. We still possess the Elim archival records (some in Swedish) of those earliest days. In the 1970s and 1980s, the Elim church graciously allowed DBC to

---

[17] The house was built by Martin Pierce (1796–1885), a New Bedford mason, in about 1829.

use their baptistery for services of believers' baptism. Elim disbanded upon merger with DBC in 1991, and its two properties, on Middle Street (the church building) and on Ocean Street (the parsonage), were sold in 1996. The parsonage had been built by Elim people in 1910 at a cost of $3,500. Today the church building on Middle Street continues in use as a church known as The Worship Center. Most of this brief Elim history has never before been published.

THE FIRST CHRISTIAN CHURCH OF HIXVILLE (1780)

With some irony, considering its beginning, DBC enjoyed a warm fellowship with the congregation at Hixville from the time of the Damgaards' coming in 1983 until the departure of then-pastor-elder Ken Harman, who left Hixville in 1991 after a seventeen-year ministry, to begin a new church in Danielson, Connecticut. An annual joint Thanksgiving Eve service began between DBC and Hixville, and the Damgaards and Harmans began their own tradition of spending Thanksgiving Day together with their families. This lasted until the Harmans eventually relocated to North Carolina in 2002. During Ken Harman's time at Hixville, he authored a fascinating summary of Hixville's long, interesting history entitled *Hixville Highlights.* Many people came to Christ and were "discipled" at Hixville in these years and the church was a very close-knit congregation. They also completed an unusual (and much needed) addition to their 135 year old building which was a great challenge for the contractor, A.P. Whitaker, and for the congregation. The resulting completion was a beautiful and historically congruent enhancement including an elevator and a new classroom wing.

In the mid 1990s two separate groups of church members departed from Hixville—some left and became part of the Bethany Gospel Chapel in Swansea and others subsequently left to begin the Emmaus Christian Church. These met at the Watuppa Grange Hall for a number of years. Subsequently, that church merged with

The Clifford Chapel (which itself was begun in 1891) on Acushnet Avenue in New Bedford and came to be known as the Emmaus Christian Church at Clifford Chapel. DBC continues to enjoy fellowship and some joint ministry with the Emmaus Church.

PACIFIC UNION CONGREGATIONAL CHURCH (1856)

Fellowship between DBC and the Pacific Union Congregational Church (PUCC) began under my ministry and that of Pastor Jeff Evans of PUCC (1988-1994.) It continued through the PUCC pastorate of Eric Nelson (1995-2000) and that of Nathan Hall (2001 to the present.) DBC was committed to being a supporting church for Nathan and Eileen Hall when they were considering missionary work in Ireland, and then when Nathan became PUCC's full-time pastor instead, the churches became closer. DBC also contributed interest and prayer support for PUCC's long-term mission project in Honduras.

MULLEIN HILL BAPTIST CHURCH (1842) AND THE MULLEIN HILL CHRISTIAN ACADEMY

Under the pastorate of Rev. Ken Nanfelt[18] and associate pastor Clint Eastman,[19] I became a good friend of Mullein Hill Baptist Church in Lakeville. Pastors Nanfelt and Eastman hosted me as a guest speaker and Bible teacher for several years in Mullein Hill on frequent Sunday evenings. Nanfelt and Eastman were responsible for bringing many

---

[18] Known for his founding of the *DelKen* Dry Cleaning chain—"Del" from Nanfelt's beloved wife, Adele, and "Ken" for himself. Adele served in DBC as a wonderful and skilled guest pianist, and Pastor Nanfelt spoke in DBC many times over the years. Ken was known also for a broad experience in evangelicalism throughout New England, including ministering as a regular vocalist for the Word of Life ministry of Jack Wyrtzen.

[19] Clint Eastman was a much-beloved minister in the region for many years and helped co-found, with Pastor Damgaard and Dr. Eric Sweitzer, the Charis Counseling Center Pastor's Group in 1990.

fine Bible scholars, some internationally known, to the area for conferences and seminars, including Gordon-Conwell Theological Seminary professors Roger Nicole, Douglas Stuart, Walter Kaiser, Raymond Pendleton, and John Jefferson Davis.

My wife, Renée, was one of the first teachers at the church's new school, Mullein Hill Christian Academy, and taught there from 1993 to 1999. I served on the school's board of directors in those same years, chairing it from 1995 until 1999, and DBC attender Victor Gonsalves also served for several years on that board. Several DBC leaders spoke in chapel for MHCA, and fundraising efforts were supported as well. Pastors Nanfelt and Eastman were also key leaders in the 1993 Franklin Graham Crusade in New Bedford. I was pleased to remain a good friend of MHBC for years after Nanfelt's and Eastman's departures, via friendship and support to MHBC leaders Jeff and Charlene Doel, Edward and Gerrie Macomber, and David and Cecile Sinclair up to the present time with their new shepherd, Pastor Kory Tedrick.

Lighthouse Assembly of God

Dartmouth Bible Church also shared occasional joint services with Lighthouse Assembly of God, which was begun in Westport in February 2004. Pastor John Costa was commissioned by Calvary Temple (Assemblies of God or AG) in Fall River—also a sister church with DBC—to begin a new A.o.G. church in Westport. DBC and Lighthouse have shared fellowship since then, and the Lighthouse church has joined in the joint services with DBC, PUCC, and Emmaus. DBC as well as Pacific Union Congregational Church (with Pastor Nathan Hall) were accommodating and helpful to the new Lighthouse fellowship and assisted them in their early months in a number of ways. Pastor John Costa is a good friend to me, and we have prayed together with Pastor Hall as well on numerous occasions.

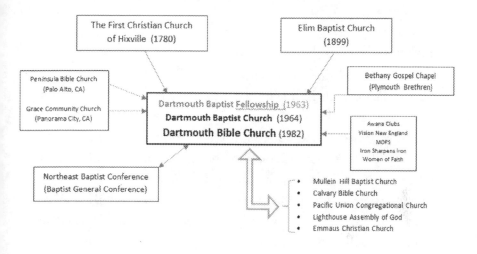

OTHER CHURCHES

Other churches in the area have partnered with us for prayer, mutual encouragement, and support of our various ministries. These include Calvary Pentecostal in East Freetown (Pastor Curtis Diaz); Calvary Temple Assembly of God in Fall River (Pastor Joe Biddle); Long Plain Baptist Church[20] in Acushnet (Pastors Stanley Decker, Art Stratton, Bob Chapman, and Hank Souza); the granddaddy of old churches in our region, the First Congregational Church on the Green in Middleboro, which dates to 1696 (Pastors Bob Pardon, Bruce Brown, James Henry, and Peter Murdy); and Calvary Bible Church in Westport (Pastors Dean Bonsall and Greg Gifford). With so few Bible churches in the region one might imagine that DBC and Calvary Bible Church would be very close. Calvary Pastors Dean Bonsall and Greg Gifford had friendly connections with DBC, but under subsequent pastors at Calvary, relations with our church became nonexistent as Calvary distanced itself from us. (More will be said about this later.)

---

[20] Long Plain Baptist is a descendant of one of six area evangelical churches planted by Elder Daniel Hix before 1838.

Joint Services

Thanksgiving Eve

Out of the friendship between myself and Mr. Ken Harman, pastor-elder of the First Christian Church of Hixville (1974–1991), the idea occurred to us to hold a joint service of Thanksgiving between the two churches in November 1984. It was held at the Hixville Church and continued without interruption until 1995 when certain changes at Hixville Church and the formation of the new Emmaus Christian Church precipitated a gulf between DBC and the Hixville church, which had become separatistically reformed. The joint service came to involve DBC and Emmaus. Due to the new friendship with Pastor Jeff Evans at the Pacific Union Congregational Church at the Head of the River in Westport, that church was added to the annual celebration, now between DBC, PUCC, and Emmaus. In 2007, the Acoaxet[21] Chapel and the new Lighthouse Assembly of God (Westport) were added to the joint service. The Dartmouth Baptist Church (now in New Bedford) also has joined this service. All of the churches possess an evangelical doctrine. A love offering is usually received at the joint service for an area outreach ministry.

Good Friday

A joint service between the churches mentioned above on Good Friday evening began in 2001. This service was modeled after a long-running daytime service of the same kind hosted for many years at the International Church of the Nazarene in New Bedford since the 1950s, in which Rev. David Schaffer and myself participated often.

---

[21] Acoaxet Chapel had been a summertime-only fellowship but became a year-round church in 2007 and is pastored by Rev. Robert Hollis, a former pastor of the Old Stone Church in Tiverton, Rhode Island. "Acoaxet" is the ancient Wampanoag native-American name for the western part of Dartmouth, Massachusetts, now Westport.

Focus is on the cross and death of Christ, and this service includes a brief message by each of several pastors and a musical contribution by someone from each of their churches.

NATIONAL DAY OF PRAYER

Joint services of prayer have been enjoyed in various configurations on the occasion of the National Day of Prayer (the first Thursday of May each year). Various ministers and pastors have participated. In 2008 I began leading a *NDP* gathering at noon on campus at UMass Dartmouth for believers there, and in 2011 DBC hosted an evening *NDP* service, including people and pastors from eight regional churches.

SISTER MINISTRIES

It has been a delight to be connected with a number of Christian ministries beyond the specific churches in the area. We have supported some of these in various ways.

THE CHRISTIAN DAY SCHOOL OF
GREATER FALL RIVER (1952–93)

DBC's connection to the Christian Day School of Greater Fall River was indirect. A number of DBC people had attended Christian Day as students, were parents of students there, or served at the school in some capacity. I was invited to serve on their board of directors in 1990, which I did until the school closed in 1993.

Other connections included Mr. Milton Reed's serving the school as a bus driver in the 1960s and attendance at the school by Craig Graham, Eric Schmidlin, and Karyn Gahan, children of DBC members Bob and Nancy Graham, Dr. Dean Schmidlin, and Brendan and Barbara Gahan. Noteworthy is Brendan Gahan's service in Christian Day as a teacher between 1980 and 1985. It was in that time that I first met Brendan, upon the latter's invitation to me to speak at Christian Day in chapel.

Sadly, Christian Day came upon difficult times in the late 1980s and was forced into bankruptcy. Their fine building, the Borden mansion on Highland Avenue, was placed on the market for sale. I had been invited to serve on a fresh and new board of directors in 1990 to attempt to save the school. The school's indebtedness was too great, however, and in the final days of evacuation by school personnel in 1993 I came upon a file cabinet in the old mansion vault in the basement. This cabinet contained the long-forgotten student records of all who had attended Christian Day since its beginning in 1952. There I discovered the elementary records of several adult Christians who were well known in the region, including those of Jonathan Donner (worship leader at DBC) and his siblings. I recovered as many of those files as I could and forwarded them to the former students. Many people in DBC were saddened at the demise of what had once been a fine institution for Christian education. Peak enrollment had reached 230 students by the mid-1980s.

Vision New England

Dating back to 1889 with the founding of the Evangelistic Association of New England, this inter-New England ministry touched thousands of lives over the decades. EANE changed their name to Vision New England in the late 1990s and at its peak in that time was the largest regional association for evangelism and renewal in the nation. The pinnacle of Vision New England's ministry each year was for many years Congress, a large weekend-long conference and celebration in Boston, attended by as many as ten thousand Christians. DBC people attended, participated, and enjoyed Congress for a number of years. DBC members also participated in and supported Vision New England through financial giving and attendance at area activities for years, including participating in the annual fall Sunday School "NEACE" conference (the New England Association for Christian Education).

IRON SHARPENS IRON

Growing out of the Promise-Keepers men's conference movement came "Iron Sharpens Iron," a ministry to Christian men still ongoing at this writing.

DBC men have enthusiastically participated in retreats and conferences sponsored by ISI, including support for various spinoff men's ministries. DBC elder Steuart Bailey, along with other

Christian men from South Coast, Massachusetts, attended *Stand in the Gap: A Sacred Assembly of Men* on October 4, 1997, when over 3 million Christian men descended on the Mall in Washington, DC, for a day of personal repentance and prayer for our nation. To my knowledge, no such gathering of that magnitude had ever occurred in the history of our nation.

"A Woman's Concern"

A network of pro-life and Christian crisis pregnancy centers opened in Massachusetts in the 1990s. One of these, called A Woman's Concern, opened in the former Borden mansion/Christian Day School on Highland Avenue in Fall River. DBC began supporting this center enthusiastically through the annual budget and through their baby-bottle fund-raiser every winter. Pro-life concerns and efforts began in DBC in 1985 when I joined the Lifeline Action Committee alongside David and Ruth Schaffer (Elim), a number of First Christian Church of Hixville members, and a number of Roman Catholic friends. Long-term support for pro-life efforts, including Holocaust remembrance events, involvement with Concerned Women for America, letter-writing, and attendance at various major pro-life rallies, has been a consistent priority of Dartmouth Bible Church into the 2000s.

Awana Clubs, International

In addition to our own church's Awana Clubs (described below), we have happily participated in regional and national events with Awana. These include Scholarship Camp, Awana Games (formerly called "Awana Olympics"), Varsity USA (now called "Summit"), and Bible Quizzing, as well as various international missions trips. DBC also has supported the regional Awana missionaries. In addition, DBC supported missionary Frank Carmical, who for a number of years was associated with development of international Awana ministries in many countries.

CHARIS COUNSELING CENTER

Charis Counseling Center in Middleboro, Massachusetts, has provided much-needed Christian counseling services to many DBC people over the years. As an outgrowth of the First Congregational Church on the Green, the Center has consistently grown in its ministry as more therapists were added to their staff. As a distinction has arisen in Christian ministry between pastoral and clinically based Christian therapy, many churches in Bristol County have appreciated the work of Charis counselors. Charis's Director, Dr. Eric Sweitzer, has spoken several times in DBC over the years and is the facilitator of a pastor's group of which I have been a member since 1990. Charis has been a reliable and helpful resource and as such is very valuable to DBC.

COMMUNITY CHAPLAIN SERVICE

Started by Rev. David Kimball, a former pastor at Elim Baptist Church, Community Chaplain Service began in the 1970s for the purpose of sharing the gospel and bringing a Christian ministry of Protestant and evangelical chaplaincy into area nursing homes. Rev. David Schaffer followed Rev. Kimball as director, and the CCS grew to a large number of chaplains in several states. DBC has supported the Schaffers in their chaplaincy and the annual CCS banquet, as well as providing our facility for training sessions for several years.

EXPANDING DBC MINISTRIES AND CONNECTIONS

In the 1990s and early 2000s, many ministries were explored and added to the overall work and outreach of Dartmouth Bible Church. As the Lord brought additional gifted, capable, and available people to the church, a wider impact and deeper internal ministry were developed. A growing church is capable of doing more and varied ministry, while a small and static church ministry—which is so typical in southern New England—is limited in what they can explore.

BOOTH MINISTRIES

An evangelistic "tabling" ministry was in place at the Hathaway Road flea market by 1982 and was also offered annually at the Whaling City Festival for several years in the 1980s. Larry Carlysle was involved at a flea market, and Michael Ponte and others were involved in staffing the Whaling City booth for three days each July. Free books, tracts, and water were the attraction, with the hope of striking up evangelistic conversations during the "tabling" or booth time. The gospel was directly shared with many people on these special occasions.

AWANA CLUBS

After considering several national children's programs, DBC made a decision in 1987 to establish an Awana Club at Dartmouth Bible Church. AWANA stands for "Approved Workmen Are Not Ashamed" (from on 2 Tim. 2:15, KJV). Based in the Chicago area and started at the North Side Gospel Center in Chicago in 1941, Awana is the an evangelical organization with fully integrated evangelism and discipleship programs for children ages—two to eighteen—that actively involve parents, church leaders, and mentors.

Each week in the overall Awana ministry more than 1.5 million children and youth, 400,000 volunteers, and 170-plus field staff take part in Awana in over 25,000 churches from over one hundred Protestant denominations in the United States and internationally.[22] The program marketed itself as being highly structured and that

---

[22] http://awana.org/about/about-history,default,pg.html.

it needed only leadership commitments and minimal training to begin. Ron Brunette agreed to serve as our first "Commander." From the second year through to the present, David Hawkins has served as Commander of DBC Awana. Eventually DBC Awana Clubs extended all the way through the senior year of high school. That club was called Varsity, then AKX, then Journey, and now "YM." At our peak, we were sending a group of senior high members to the national Varsity USA each year in Chicago, Omaha, and other cities. Other clubbers joined international missions trips with Awana (to Russia, Romania, etc.), and many attended the Awana regional summer camps. Several DBC clubbers achieved Awana's highest award, the *Citation* Award—having successfully memorized six hundred Bible verses and completed many study books and other accomplishments.

- Six individuals to date have completed the *Citation* award. These include Heather Crossman (1999), Jocelyn Damgaard (2000), Susanna Damgaard (2003), Kerry Hand (2003), Tina Randall (2004), and Billy Hawkins (2008).
- Twelve clubbers to date have completed Awana's second-highest award (the *Meritorious* award). They are Jocelyn Damgaard (1997), Sonja Aanensen (1998), Donna Wingrove (1998), Heather Crossman (1999), Susanna Damgaard (1999), Tina Randall (2000), Dominic Zarecki (2001), Katie Hand (2003), Billy Hawkins (2004), Alexander Zarecki (2004), Stephen Hawkins (2006), and Brianne Cihak (2011).
- Since 1995, twenty-one clubbers have completed Awana's third-highest award, the *Timothy* award.

In May 2012, DBC Awana Clubs finished the season with forty clubbers regularly attending, and in the 2011–12 season, more joined them as the Chinese Bible study met concurrently with Awana. Many DBC members and a number of nonmembers and friends from outside DBC have assisted in many ways over the years to make Awana one of the church's most vital and consistent programs. The Word of God is center-stage in Awana, along with Bible memorization and exposure to various biblical and theological themes. The 2012–2013 season will be Awana's twenty-fifth year at DBC. God has blessed us in countless ways.

COFFEE HOUSE

Originally the DBC Coffee House was called "The Alternative." Leaders had become familiar with a weekly Christian coffee house in Norton, Massachusetts, called "The Ark," and a few DBC people attended there each Saturday night. This was where DBC people originally met musician Dominick DeLuca, who became a long-time friend of DBC. Musicians were scheduled, and "The Alternative" was underway at DBC in 1982. The Coffee House went through many variations and reconfigurations. At one point in the mid-1990s, the DBC Coffee House was offered weekly with the main auditorium being transformed by a team of volunteers stacking the pews, setting up the coffee house environment and preparing food. Several people have served as key leaders, namely Larry Carlysle, Jon Donner, David Cadieux and most recently Paul Roy. Since 2004 the "Damascus Road" Coffee House has consistently provided a monthly ministry of Christian music, fellowship, and relaxation under Paul Roy's leadership and love for this work. Few have taken their personal calling to ministry more wholeheartedly than has Paul. He has recruited many fine musicians and bands over these years, from all over New England.

MOTHERS OF PRE-SCHOOLERS (MOPS)

DBC began a chapter of the national ministry of MOPS in 2009 under the leadership of Megan Whitlow and short-term DBC attender Winnie Lee (who subsequently relocated to San Diego).

This outreach ministry to young mothers has grown slowly and provides an effective outreach to un-churched as well as Christian mothers. DBC has appreciated Megan's vision and effort to get MOPS off the ground! We hope to recruit and train more leaders and to see MOPS become a long-standing and effective outreach of DBC for years to come.

Chapter 4

Significant Changes

And whatsoever ye do in word or deed, do all
in the name of the Lord Jesus, giving thanks to
God and the Father by Him. (Col. 3:17)

Change Is Inevitable

We always hope that the important things in a church do not change: the exposition of the Word of God, the hunger for hearing the Lord's voice together as a congregation, a deeply felt mutual care and discipleship process among the members, and a passion to share the gospel with the lost. Change does occur, though, and if we look back into the first twenty years of DBC's history, we can see a few notable changes. First, the church changed from a small group meeting in a home to a larger small group meeting in the VFW hall. When the church built its first building, the church body grew again, and the church inevitably became more stable and more able to expand its ministry. This occurred under the pastorate of Jim Harding.

As the 1960s turned into the 1970s, the church gradually added younger people and developed a strong desire for change—this time from a traditional Baptist church model toward a more *progressively* biblical philosophy of ministry. This resulted in the departure of most of the older church members and a shift to a younger style of ministry, which came to define the church. How this is interpreted varies with who is doing the interpreting. Clearly though, the shift occurred. When I first learned about DBC while I was still in Dallas, one document that I saw was entitled "Dartmouth Bible Church" and another "Dartmouth Baptist Church" which was a little confusing. When I arrived, DBC still had the feel of changing and discarding older methods of ministry for newer ones. We had come to Dartmouth from a Plymouth Brethren church in Dallas, so the sympathies of the new DBC leaders were not unfamiliar to us. At the same time, we had no axe to grind about more traditional or formal church polity, having been trained and ordained in a Reformed church and discipled in Baptist-type churches before that. It was not until the merger with Elim Baptist Church in 1991 that DBC finally started to shed the feeling of tension between the "old school" and "new school" transition. The merger put a whole new game on the table, as happened again after the new facility was constructed in 1999.

DREAMS OF EXPANDING

With the clear need to find more space, DBC began to dream and pray about expanding. I had become friends with contractor Al Whitaker of Raynham. Whitaker, a member of Central Baptist Church in Middleboro, had built a number of church buildings in the area. He utilized the "design-build" concept in facility design and construction, and offered to provide a basic concept to DBC without cost. I met with Whitaker and his architect, Robert Shaw, and they provided several concept drawings that envisioned a large addition to the existing building on Morton Avenue. Bob Whitlow and I then constructed a large model of the facility and unveiled it at a "vision banquet" hosted by the church in the fall of 1990. The banquet was held in the Campus Center Sunset Room at UMass Dartmouth. It was a hopeful time for the church.

Model built by Bob Whitlow and Neil Damgaard,
on Whitaker concept, in 1990

MERGER TALKS WITH ELIM BAPTIST CHURCH

None of us had ever been a part of a merger between two churches, nor had we known anyone else who had undertaken such an endeavor. Our merger with Elim Baptist Church began on July 3, 1990, when I was invited for coffee at the Dartmouth Friendly's restaurant by Elim's pastor, Lou Parascand (Louis J. Parascand Jr., MDiv, from Gordon-Conwell Theological Seminary). At that meeting Lou casually asked me, "How's your building program going?" Lou knew that DBC had been exploring and dreaming about adding on to our small facility for several years. I told him that Whitaker had provided us with a couple of good concept drawings. He replied, "Well, maybe we can help you with that."

Lou had been a pastoral friend of mine since his arrival at Elim in 1987. Elim had undertaken a serious evaluation of their future and formed the "Crossroad Committee" to determine a plan encompassing all possibilities for revitalizing the church. They explored four options: moving their location out of downtown New Bedford, transforming their church body into an intentional "urban mission" style church, an outright closure, or a merger with some existing area church of like spirit and mission. They contacted several area churches. On that that day in Friendly's, Pastor Lou informed me of their plans.

The idea sounded attractive to me, although, as it turned out, DBC was the only church that would even talk to them about a merger. Lou indicated that he expected Elim would bring to a merger several hundred thousand dollars' worth of assets (their two properties plus furnishings, etc.) and however many Elim members would be willing to transfer their membership into a merged church. On July 4, I informed Bob Whitlow of the idea at our church picnic. Bob was intrigued, and in the weeks to follow, with much prayer, meetings of introduction between leaders from both churches occurred regarding a possible merger. The next step, which happened in September, was to form a joint committee. There were many questions to be answered. We also carefully informed our respective members of the possibility of merger, and they were invited to pray and to vigorously join in the discussions. We wanted no one in either congregation to feel coerced into this venture.

David and Ruth Schaffer were still Elim members and attendees. The Schaffers had become good family friends of the Damgaards and had been supportive of us since September of 1983, just after we had arrived in Dartmouth. David had served as Elim's pastor from 1972 until 1987, when he resigned the pastorate in order to begin working with the Community Chaplain Service.

After much prayer, the following details toward merger were agreed upon:

1. The merger would commence with a trial period.
2. Prayer would be the glue of any decisions to merge.
3. Lou Parascand would become the new Associate Pastor for

Discipleship in the merged church, with equal preaching time in the beginning, to phase down over a period of time to occasional preaching.

4. Since Elim would cease to exist, its affiliation with the Baptist General Conference would be terminated. Conference officials graciously accommodated this wish, and there were no outstanding loans. (This graciousness stands in contrast to the experience of at least one local Episcopal church in more recent years that, upon seeking dissolution with their denomination, had to surrender the keys to their building.)

5. Elim properties would immediately be put on the market for sale, and when sales were completed, a fund for an eventual down-payment on a home for the Parascands would be established from the proceeds of sale.

6. Double worship services would begin in order to accommodate the enlarged congregation, and all ministries would be held at the Dartmouth location.

7. Elim officers would be considered for inclusion in the DBC structure, but no automatic postings would be enacted.

8. All assets would be legally merged into the existing DBC corporation.

9. An updated Constitution and By Laws would be authored along with specific policy statements for existing ministries and procedures.

10. A church growth and strategic plan would be formulated as soon as possible.

REVEREND LOUIS J. PARASCAND JR., M.DIV.

Rev. Louis Parascand Jr. was hired to be the pastor of Elim Baptist Church in New Bedford in 1987. Over the next six months of discussion between our churches, Lou's good leadership contributed to the merger between the two churches. Parascand became DBC's Associate Pastor for Discipleship and worked on several projects, including development of a spiritual gifts exploration and implementation program, which he called *GiftLINK*. Seminars and counseling were provided to church members in this area of the Christian life, with a number of mature members helping. After three years in DBC, Lou sought and found a new ministry as Senior Pastor of Faith Community Church (EFCA) in Waupaca, Wisconsin, where he, his wife, Janie, and their five children—Alison, Louis, Katie, Mandy-Grace, and Seth—moved in April 1994. The Parascands ministered there until 2008, when they retired from professional ministry and relocated to San Diego, California.

MERGER WITH ELIM BAPTIST CHURCH OF NEW BEDFORD

Merger between Dartmouth Bible Church and Elim Baptist Church began its trial period on the first Sunday of January 1991. The trial period came to its conclusion successfully, and full merger was voted in by both memberships at the quarterly meeting on the third Sunday evening of April 1991. At the time, we hardly understood the very significant changes this merger would impose upon us all. While the feelings of "us" and "them" gradually diminished over the first five years, some feeling of sorrow would linger at what had been lost. This was true with some of the people from Elim and understandably so. A number of the long-term Elim members simply could not adjust to the idea of a merger and therefore did not come to Dartmouth. Others, though, notably Phil and Emma Griffin, Ruth Burns (who would turn one hundred years old before too long after the merger), Ray St. Don, and Irene Kvilhaug, bravely stepped off one ship and on to another. They were inspirational to us all for their cheerfulness and determination to see what God had planned for the next chapter! As new people came into the joined congregation, this helped to diminish the sad feeling. By 1996 and the commencement of a serious new building program, the change from the old DBC and Elim had become permanent. DBC inherited Elim's communion table, a wonderful Yamaha baby grand piano (purchased in 1981), a communion service, and classic sterling silver tea service, used for many years in Elim's "parlor."

Small Groups Ministries and Philosophy

Since the early 1980s, small groups have replaced the traditional Wednesday night prayer meeting in DBC's ministry philosophy. For some people this was a big change, but it was also a national trend. Small groups are envisioned to be of several types, but all are designed to provide a closer fellowship and friendship between members, with an emphasis on prayer still included.

Bible Studies

Many small group Bible studies have been enjoyed in DBC over the years, a number meeting in people's homes. A hunger for the Word of God does not lessen, especially when new people and new Christians are regularly enfolded into the church. Small group leadership training has also been offered periodically.

Prayer Groups

Nothing is more important than prayer, and over the decades, prayer has often been enjoyed in small prayer groups. At one time the midweek prayer meeting was the main focus for prayer, but in recent decades, smaller and more intimate prayer fellowships have sprung up. Sometimes the focus is missions support, sometimes on the need for personal sanctification, and other times the focus is aimed at supporting our children. Every church ministry team meeting opens and closes with prayer. As well, seeking the Lord for revival, both national and local, has often moved DBC people in prayer.

Fellowship Groups

Sometimes the need for closer fellowship has stimulated the formation of small fellowship groups, where the goal is to provide Christian warmth, friendship, and even fun. For several years in the late 1990s, a number of DBC people enjoyed their own bowling league on Sunday afternoons, celebrated with a year-end banquet and trophies. The late elder Frank Sinclair (d. 2001) and his wife, Madeline, were instrumental in facilitating this league. For three summers, DBC enjoyed having a softball team. There has also been a men's camera club for several years and currently a fantasy football league (begun by Jonathan Marginson in 2009). Renée and I have led several couples' fellowship groups. Other church members have hosted fellowships in their homes to provide friendship and warmth. The need for connection and camaraderie is timeless, and DBC has always looked for ways to provide and enhance meaningful fellowship.

LC's Men's Ministry

A monthly breakfast with devotions began in 1994 for men over fifty years old. It was well received, and other regular social activities were added. A "Ladies Appreciation Night" was started, with a special dinner prepared and served by the men themselves. This has taken place on the Saturday evening before Mother's Day every year since then. It has been vivaciously emceed by Brendan Gahan and has been an event that many women have looked forward to. An annual excursion to a Pawtucket Red Sox baseball game has been enjoyed, and many men have attended. The LCs also have sponsored their own missions fund, from which they supported various missions projects. Leadership as well as vision for this ministry was provided by Brendan Gahan, John Zarecki, and Larry Logan. The breakfasts themselves were prepared and served by Ruth Schaffer, Elizabeth Zarecki, and other beloved wives.

SWAT (SENIOR WOMEN ALONE TOGETHER), 1992–2010

Lou Parascand initiated a senior women's fellowship centered on Bible study and companionship in 1992, just after merger with Elim. Elim had had a long-standing senior women's ministry called "Missions Circle" dating back to the early twentieth century. At the time of the merger, several women inquired as to whether a senior women's ministry would be continued in the new merged church. Lou facilitated this new ministry with DBC's founding pastor's wife, Ruth Durfee Nolan, as leader. It continued for eighteen years until late 2010, when it was put on hiatus due to Ruth Nolan's health needs. Her ministry was greatly appreciated, and it was a fitting testimony to the goodness of the Lord and a determined spirit to keep the Word of God central in the lives of Christians, regardless of age or situation. It is hoped that SWAT can be reconvened soon.

ACCOUNTABILITY GROUPS

Bob Whitlow and other men sensed a need to set up men's accountability groups, beginning in 2008. The idea was to provide an intimate and secure way for men to share their struggles and minister to one another. Three groups began, and the possibility of starting a women's group was also explored.

TASK GROUPS

From time to time, the need for task groups also arose, which are team ministries associated with particular needs in the church.

The most notable of these has been the New Building Committee (1991–2001). This group met tirelessly to plan for and carry out the construction of a new building and a reengineered design for our grounds. It included Bob Whitlow, Bob Graham, Kathie Marginson, Sylvia Morris, John Zarecki, and myself, and it was chaired by Barbara Gahan. The group happily disbanded in 2001 after the completion of the interior spaces by DBC volunteers. Most were still present when the mortgage was paid off and ceremonially burned in 2008.

Other task groups have included a finance team, a buildings and grounds team, a short-lived "special events team," a "make-ready" group in support of the *Mobile Loaves & Fishes* van based out of St. Paul's Methodist Church, a library group, Nursery support group for MOPS, staff-search teams, and special committees to draft various DBC documents and policies. Explorations began in 2012 to create a small "personnel" team to assist with employee-related business matters and a "safety team" to create a safety plan and related protocols for the DBC facility.

REJOINING THE BAPTIST GENERAL CONFERENCE

In 1993 I began to sense a need to find some larger group or association with which to formally affiliate. I actually had never been part of any formal affiliation since becoming a Christian, but in addition to the need to for find a denominational health insurance plan for our staff, there was also the strong feeling that maturity as a church could be nurtured by a meaningful affiliation. To me it seemed logical that if there was anything we could do as a body that might enhance our church life by, say, 2 percent, why would we decline that possibility?

The idea ran against the independent-mindedness of many of our people and also against bad experiences some members had undergone with denominational hierarchies. The notion of being linked to churches far away from Dartmouth with whom we would rarely share any frequent fellowship also weighed somewhat against the idea. Nonetheless, our leaders considered the Evangelical Free Church of America (and met once with their regional representative), the Christian Missionary Alliance Church, and (briefly) the Independent Fundamental Churches of America. Associate Pastor Parascand gently suggested that even though both DBC and Elim had earlier withdrawn from the Baptist General Conference, a reinvestigation of the BGC might reveal attractive changes of their philosophy of ministry. In early 1993, Pastor Parascand introduced me to Ron Larsen, who was then the District Executive Minister of the Northeast Baptist Conference, as well as to his Assistant District Executive Minister Paul Hubley.

With much prayer and after learning that the Conference did offer a health insurance plan to Conference pastors, DBC applied for acceptance into the Northeast Baptist Conference of the Baptist General Conference. Many Conference priorities seemed to be matched to what were now our own. The good spirit and more open and progressive leadership of the Conference were attractive, and in 1994 DBC was formally accepted as a Conference church (without requiring a name change). I subsequently served with new District Executive Minister Paul Hubley as a trustee of the district for six years. Within a couple of years, the health insurance plan offered by the Conference was discontinued, but DBC continued a happy affiliation and participation in the district as much as possible, including financial support to both the district and the national Conference. Delegates were sent to the annual meeting of the district in Hartford occasionally, including John Zarecki, David and Jennifer Cadieux, and Steuart and Carol Bailey. My wife, Renée, and I also attended two annual district meetings in Hartford. (In the early 1980s, Russell Viera served as a delegate as well.) The Conference and the New England district changed their names to Converge

Worldwide and Converge Northeast in 2009. There are about eighty churches in our district throughout the Northeast and about one thousand churches worldwide with which we are connected through Converge Worldwide.

THE FRANKLIN GRAHAM CRUSADE

In 1992 Franklin Graham, the son of evangelist Billy Graham, was invited and was willing to consider a five-night crusade at the Zeiterion Theatre in New Bedford upon inquiry by Reverends Ken Nanfelt and Clint Eastman and a committee of numerous area pastors. The October 1993 Franklin Graham Crusade was the largest and most comprehensive collaborative Christian effort in Greater New Bedford in recent memory. DBC was one of about sixty participating churches (including supportive observers from the Greek Orthodox Church and the Catholic Diocese of Fall River) in the yearlong period of preparation and prayer before the crusade, to be held that October. There had not been a region-wide evangelistic campaign of this magnitude since the visit by Dwight L. Moody to New Bedford for four weeks in 1895.

DBC's Associate Pastor Lou Parascand served on the main committee for planning, and people from the recently merged DBC/Elim congregation contributed support and effort for the crusade. Pastor Ken Nanfelt of Mullein Hill Baptist Church in Lakeville—a great friend of all evangelical churches in the area—was the crusade's chairman. During the five-day crusade, some six hundred people recorded commitments to Christ, including New Bedford residents John and Elizabeth Zarecki, with whom I had visited and formed a friendship. Subsequent efforts to lure other well-known evangelists to New Bedford have failed, underscoring the specialness of the 1993 crusade.

Elevator Project

It may seem like a mundane and forgettable detail, but in the days it was happening, the need for an elevator posed a daunting challenge! In the summer and fall of 1993, DBC planned and constructed a handicapped access elevator and enclosure—the first on-site construction since 1968. Architect Dan Lewis from Southborough was hired, and Bob Graham and Associate Pastor Lou Parascand personally carried out the construction. The design anticipated an eventual addition to the building and would service both buildings. Several permits were required, along with a variance to install a residential-style "Elevette" product instead of a commercial elevator, which would have cost twice as much. Architect Lewis argued before the Massachusetts Access and Elevator Boards in Boston with a logic stating that since DBC was seeking to provide an enhancement to an existing facility, it should be granted the variances, which were subsequently granted. The construction project was Pastor Parascand's final project as a member of staff at DBC before his resignation in October of 1993.

One special detail: as part of the elevator project, a large concrete handicap access ramp with cast iron railings was constructed by Bob Graham and Joe Tavares on the north side of the building in 1994. After years of physically lifting wheelchair-bound member Nancy Graham into the building every Sunday, the ramp and elevator were a source of great encouragement. This was dramatically removed upon construction of the new building just five years later. (I stood and watched ambivalently as a large excavator tore it apart in just a couple of hours when construction on the new building finally began.) What in 1994 seemed like an impressive addition was dwarfed by the magnitude of the overall expansion in 1999. The large and heavy railings were sold for scrap in 1999. When the contractor's large excavator broke up the ramp, I remember thinking, *"This was the most short-lived major concrete project I have ever seen!*

Sale of Elim Properties

While we awaited a sale of the church property, the newly merged church decided to grant a request from the Greater Miracle Deliverance Church for rental of the Elim church building. Officials of that church agreed to provide a monthly contribution and to maintain the condition of the church, as well as its security. The relationship for lasted about one year, until GMDC no longer needed the facility.

Three and a half years later, purchasers were found for the two Elim properties: the church on Middle Street, which included the historic Pierce House, and the parsonage on Ocean Street. This seemed like a long wait, but it provided DBC with the time to really think through the details of what we wanted in a new facility. As we waited, we learned patience and the value of keeping our eyes on our main ministry: people. In the interim, we considered a viable if somewhat unorthodox and alternative septic system, calling for the use of "Clivus-Multrum" composting toilets. This approach had been approved and was in use in other towns in Massachusetts in areas where septic conditions were problematic. Ultimately the Town of Dartmouth announced that town sewage would soon be installed on our street, and while the two-year delay was frustrating, we saw the Lord providing for us.

FINDING AN ARCHITECT
AND A CONTRACTOR

Several architects were interviewed, and DBC hired Brown & Lindquist of Yarmouth, Massachusetts, as our architectural firm. Peter Brown was the chief architect. At one early point in our relationship with Peter, while he was paying a visit to our Morton Avenue property, he mentioned that he had "had a little piece of involvement" with the construction of the original SMU campus in the 1960s. Nothing more was said of it. It was not until 2007 when I purchased the just-released *History of the University of Massachusetts at Dartmouth* that we learned that Peter had served as *lead* architect on the whole original design of the main campus of SMU, for Desmond and Lord Architects. It was a special detail that he also provided the design for the new DBC addition. It is worthy of notation in the Town's history.

In October of 2008, design plans were far enough along for the project to be offered for bids from interested contractors. I was present at the Brown & Lindquist offices when the bids came in. Seven contractors placed bids for the project, and the clear choice was Coastal Restoration & Development Corporation of Plymouth, Massachusetts, whose bid was $100,000 lower than any of the others. Late that same afternoon, Peter Brown informed me that a "Coastal" church project was underway just up the road from the Brown & Lindquist offices and that it would be good to stop by and see their work that very day. I visited the project site—Christ Chapel in Centerville—and introduced myself to several "Coastal" employees. I told them that their company had just won our contract and they were of course very friendly and interested in our project.

CONSTRUCTION OF THE ADDITION

Barbara Gahan was chairperson of our Building Committee, and its members were Bob Graham, Kathie Marginson, Sylvia Morris, Bob Whitlow, and John Zarecki. The strengths and gifts of each committee member became clear and much appreciated throughout construction. Citizen's Bank provided the construction loan, and ground was broken in April of 1999. Pre-construction preparations began in December of 1998 with the removal of the original oil tank. On that day, I thought, "this is finally happening," fifteen years after my arrival in Dartmouth. Construction was completed in the beginning of the next December, and our first service in the new sanctuary was December 12, 1999. I served as the on-site representative for DBC during construction and learned many things about construction and its process. Several details of that process deserve mention:

- On the first day of excavation (April), the contractor discovered that our soil was unsuitable for building due to its composition of fill and refuse from what we learned was the original SMTI construction in 1964. Our site was used as a convenient dumping ground by Carter Brothers Excavating during SMU's original construction (as told to me by Sonny Carter), an ironic tie to the university. This setback added $42,000 more to our project, and it was an emotional jolt.

- As construction progressed, the process of change orders to the original estimate was inevitable. Consequently, we needed to "back out" several originally planned aspects for our project, including the addition of central air-conditioning, a circular driveway on the Morton Avenue side, and a higher grade of windows and doors. These adjustments for cost were made. In retrospect, the savings of $5,000 for air conditioning was eclipsed by the $20,000 it cost us through contracting with a new firm to provide this only one year later. It only took one summer without air conditioning to convince us to add it. I also regretted that we did not add the circular driveway, as it would have been a useful enhancement to the Morton Avenue entrance. At the time I felt it would be a "hard sell" to the church family later and would appear to be a frivolous extravagance. This has proved to be true. Overall cost of original construction, not including subsequent costs in 2000 and 2001 to complete the interior spaces, was around $755,000. Our construction loan amount was approximately $260,000.

- DBC members contributed significantly in carpentry skills, labor, and finances once we got underway with construction. This is an important lesson: people *will* help once they see a project is actually occurring.

- Another important maxim we heard that has proved true for us: a new building *does* attract new people. DBC doubled in numerical size over the first ten years after construction, much of this due to the larger facility and the added ministry capability provided by expansion of the physical plant.

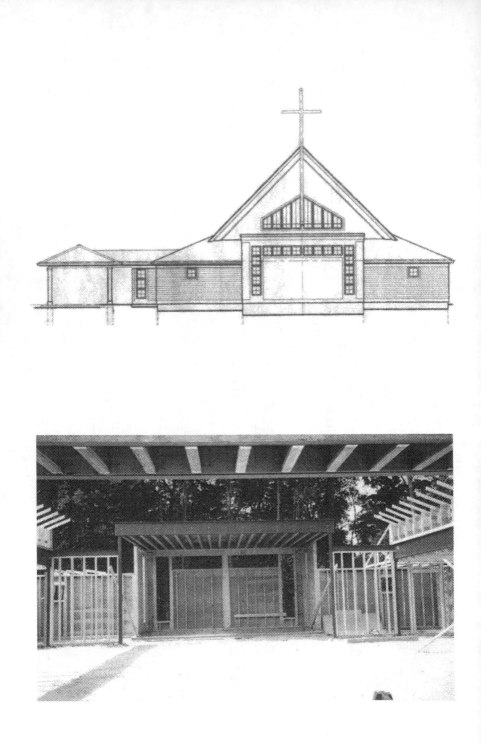

Completed "Addition," January 2000

First worship service in the new Dartmouth Bible Church sanctuary   December 12th, 1999
Keep yourselves in the love of God, waiting anxiously for the mercy of our Lord Jesus Christ to eternal life.

Many churches have built buildings, often beginning with meager resources and little more than faith and a conviction that somehow God will provide. In this, our experience was not unique. Also, it is often said among pastors, "Most of us have one building in us" because it usually takes so much out of a pastor to see a project through. I learned so much in that time, however, that I feel there's another one inside of me someplace! It was a great privilege to participate in such a project at least once. The members and regular attenders at DBC were very thankful when we gained occupancy of our new facility, and I remember much enthusiasm, hard work, and an urgency to complete the interior spaces ourselves. When I took occupancy of my new office and we hired Lynn Brown as secretary in July 2001, it felt like a new threshold was before us. The final worship service held in the old building was on Sunday, December 5, 1999. The guest speaker was Rev. Sandy Young, my life-long friend who came to DBC for a Bible Conference that weekend. Services commenced in the new sanctuary the following Sunday, December 12, 1999.

Mr. Paul Souza

Paul Souza was raised in Dartmouth and began attending DBC in 1987 upon invitation by his Agway coworker Madeline Sinclair (a DBC member).

Paul had been introduced to the gospel while working at Agway in New Bedford, at which Madeline's husband, Frank, also worked. Madeline took an interest in Paul, and through their many discussions, Paul made a commitment to Christ in 1985. In 1987 he began attending DBC and also brought his fiancée, Christine Despres. Paul became a member of DBC, and in time, Christine did as well, having made her own wonderful profession of faith. I baptized both of them, and I was privileged to perform their wedding ceremony in 1989 at the First Church of the Nazarene.

(In those days, DBC was only adequate in size to accommodate the smallest weddings.) Christine's parents, Fred and Jackie Despres, also attended DBC for a couple of years.

Mr. Paul Souza

Paul began to work with the youth of the church as a volunteer in 1998, along with Cindy Andrade (who came into DBC with the Elim members). In the years that followed, Paul developed an increasing interest in youth ministry and began to really lead in youth ministry around 2000. In 2001 Paul was hired part-time as our youth pastor and then transitioned to full-time work as our youth pastor in 2002. This ministry prospered until August 2004, when we thought Paul would begin attending Dallas Seminary. After Dallas Seminary professor Dr. John Reed made a visit to DBC, Paul was encouraged to make application to Dallas Seminary's certificate program. Although his application was accepted, Paul and Chris determined to stay in Bristol County.

Paul remained on staff at DBC until May 2005, when he returned to landscaping and agricultural work. Paul and Christine were blessed with three wonderful children, Adam, Jordan, and Jesse. Paul also invited his brother, Wayne, and Wayne's wife, Jeannette, into DBC, and they became valued and loved members until 2005, when they relocated to Virginia. Paul was DBC's first paid youth worker, and his successful ministry led DBC to continue to hire staff for youth work for years to follow. He also possessed a wonderful gift of acting and presented several dramatic presentations that were very effective. Christine has also been a blessing in DBC and served for several years as Sunday school coordinator.

MR. & MRS. THOMAS BROWN

In the winter of 2005, DBC organized and focused on the search for a new youth pastor.

We decided to look outside of the church membership, and many résumés were acquired, telephone interviews were conducted, references were checked, and prayers were engaged. The result was the selection of Mr. Tom Brown from Pennsylvania (a graduate of Lancaster Bible College), who became our next staff person—Minister of Youth and Christian Education (M.Y.C.E.) Tom and his wife, Holly, arrived at DBC in the summer of 2006, and Holly soon delivered their first child, Abigail. Daughter Sarah was born to Tom and Holly as well in the next year. After purchasing a home on Washington Street in Fairhaven, Tom and Holly ministered well among us until the family's relocation to Washington Boro, Pennsylvania, in August 2009 when Tom was called to serve as Pastor of Youth and Christian Education at Central Manor Church. The Browns became beloved to several families in the church and made a good impact on a number of DBC teens. Several teens with whom Tom worked were baptized by him that summer of 2009 at the home of Ron and Susan Brunette.

Mr. Tom and Holly Brown

Neil C. Damgaard

Miss Natasha Ferro

In the same month as the Browns' relocation, coincidentally Natasha Ferro sent an e-mail to me and inquired about the opening for working with youth in DBC. Natasha was known to DBC before she attended Messiah College.

Miss Natasha Ferro

She had attended our senior high school Awana Club (called Varsity at that time) while she was a New Bedford High School student. Since the staff need in DBC was immediate, I was happy to chat with Natasha informally over coffee. While DBC had not had a female staff member before, I was sufficiently impressed with Natasha to decide to set up an impromptu and still unofficial meeting with the elders, after which followed official interviews with a special committee, the teens themselves, and finally a group of parents of DBC youth. She was presented before the church with the recommendation to hire her as full-time "Youth and Christian Education Associate,". She was voted in and began work on November 1, 2009, in that capacity. Natasha was raised in a very fine Christian family from New Bedford and has continued to bless our church and many other area Christians in many ways. She is very much loved and appreciated by the DBC congregation, and her job title was advanced to Youth and Christian Education Director in November 2012.

Chapter 5

MORE MINISTRIES

Let love be without dissimulation. Abhor that which is evil; cleave to that which is good. Be kindly affectioned to one another with brotherly love; in honor preferring one another, not slothful in business, fervent in spirit, serving the Lord; rejoicing in hope, patient in tribulation, continuing instant in prayer, distributing to the needs of the saints, given to hospitality. (Rom. 12:9–13)

Additional ministries and fresh ways to utilize spiritual gifts are explored and developed in churches all the time! This chapter gives a brief survey of some of the ministries DBC has had in more recent years. Many large-scale and ongoing ministries are carried out by one team or another, and sometimes multiple teams collaborate on projects.

SERVING MINISTRIES

It is a normal thing for a Christian to desire to serve the body and the wider community in positive ways. We love to be looked at as a blessing, and some "serving" ministries have included the following.

Work Days

Work Days almost seem like a given in churches, but DBC has enjoyed volunteer labor for countless tasks many times over the years. Members and attenders come out to fix, clean, build, landscape, and inventory and to fellowship while doing all those things. A fellowship lunch is usually enjoyed by the workers, and much is accomplished that otherwise would wait. Work days have also provided father-son and mother-daughter experiences over the years.

Pacesetters

This group met in 1989 and 1990 for the purpose of praying over and discussing the goals and plans of our church. It is providential that we had such a group in light of the July 1990 start of merger talks with Elim. This group included myself, John Aanensen, Audie and Wendy Brockel, Chris Ferguson, Cheryl Gallegos, Milton Reed, Dean Schmidlin, and Bob and Joan Whitlow.

Building Committees

Several building committees have served over the years, with two actually overseeing construction projects in 1966–68 and 1991–2001. Serving on a building committee takes much patience and flexibility as changes and adaptations in the planning and expectations force us to walk closely with the Lord! Tempers can flare, patience is tried, and personal preferences are filtered and processed. Building committees are one of the most time-intensive but also most exciting opportunities for people in a church to experience. We are grateful for the innumerable hours devoted by building committee members over the years, both those who saw the fruit of their labor and the others who dreamed. We hope we shall again need to convene one!

YOUTH SERVICE PROJECTS

Our youth groups have often shared their arms and legs with service projects of many kinds. Each youth minister has brought his or her own particular brand of creativity, and DBC has benefited from its youth's willingness to serve. Most recently (2012), four DBC young people, accompanied by three senior women, travelled to Fairbanks, Alaska, to serve at Camp Li-Wa for two weeks on a work trip. The trip was hard work but educational and a great example of body life taken into service.

MOBILE LOAVES AND FISHES VAN TEAM

St. Paul's Methodist Church has a longtime member named George Bailey who is a fine Christian and a friend of a number of DBC families. George let us know that their church would be obtaining a "Mobile Loaves and Fishes" van to use in feeding homeless people in New Bedford. The van distributes food, clothing, gospel literature, and Bibles, all without cost, at designated locations in the city. When the new van arrived from Texas and a new pastor was installed St. Paul's (Pastor Ken MacMillen), DBC began to share in this ministry by providing a "make ready" team to prepare the van for its weekly excursions. Tom and Kathie Marginson led this team, beginning in 2011.

GROWING OUR TEAM PHILOSOPHY

It has been a deliberate and also a natural effort to join together in teams with focused ministry at heart. DBC currently (2012) has fifteen teams, up from three in 1983.

THE BOARD OF ELDERS AND THE ELDER-ADVISORS

From the time of Mel Longtin's pastorate, DBC began to transition to an elder form of government, which introduced the idea of a plurality of shepherding leaders and governors. The office of elder derives directly from multiple mentions of it in the New Testament (occurring variously as "elder," "bishop" and "shepherd") and is the most prominent church office mentioned there, after the office of "apostle." DBC decided to limit service in the office of elder to males as because this is the pattern of the New Testament. However, the ministry of "elder-advisors" was created for several Christian women in DBC in the mid-1990s in order to give the elders the benefit of their maturity and perspective. The transition to "elders" was slow, as traditionally aligned Baptist churches do not usually use the term "elder" except as applied to the office of "pastor." Also, an elder form of government is not a perfect polity and must be "grown" and in a church's developing ministry. No Christian man maintains a perfect walk with the Lord. However, over the years a number of men were found who were both willing and generally qualified to serve as *elders* and who did so faithfully and with great blessing to the body of Christ at DBC.

- Rev. John Fernandez (1981), Rev. Dr. Neil Damgaard (1983–present), Michael Martin (1984–85, resigned), Bob Whitlow (1985; 1992–2008, resigned), Dr. Dean Schmidlin (1997–2009, relocated to North Carolina and resigned), Brendan Gahan (1997–2000, retired and given *emeritus* recognition thereafter), Frank Sinclair (1997–2001, deceased July 2001), Lou Parascand (1991–1994, relocated to Wisconsin and resigned), Steuart Bailey (1997–present), Paul Hsia (2000–2005, resigned), John Zarecki (2002–present), Donald Clapp (2002–present), Rev. William Stack (2008–present), Dr. Larry Logan (2008–present), and William Hallett Jr., a charter member of DBC and a deacon in earlier years consented to serve as an elder also (2009–present). Several others served as elders-in-training for a season.

- **Elder-Advisors** (1995–1997): Emma Griffin, Barbara Gahan, and Ruth Schaffer. This was a position we created to empower and utilize a few of the more mature and experienced Christian women in our congregation as an auxiliary to the elders. For those two years, their work and contributions were much appreciated by the elders.

Elders in DBC are not elected officers. They are appointed after substantial training and affirmation by the body in a ceremony of "laying on of hands." Our practice is to always be open and observant for men with a heart for shepherding who have the time available and the required spiritual maturity. Each elder brings his own walk with the Lord and his own love for what God is doing through DBC. Ministry as a team involves utilizing the strengths of each elder and developing a mutual feeling of friendship and support between them. Differing personalities also make for a good board of elders, with some bringing a more meditative way about them and others providing a lighter touch, with humor and a bit of "whimsy," as Brendan Gahan once put it. The elders have great affection for each other and consider it a privilege to serve in this capacity. Their hearts are characterized by a love for the church body and a great burden to pray for it and support it with their own spiritual gifts.

THE BOARD OF DEACONS BECOMES THE DIACONATE

With the reintroduction of serving deaconesses alongside the deacons, the Board of Deacons became the "Diaconate," derived from the ancient Greek word for deacon, "diakonos." Actually, DBC had deaconesses as well as deacons in the early years, but this office was suspended in the late 1970s. Originally the deacons were the main leaders of the church and served as such for the first fifteen years. Currently the Diaconate is charged with watching out for the physical needs of the people of DBC. The board maintains a fund for granting financial assistance to DBC people, to which members are invited to contribute. This fund has been a blessing to many over the years.

Some seventy-seven people served DBC faithfully and capably over the years on the Diaconate, and several served as chairmen. (See Appendix 2.) Notably Shirley Barboza has served the Diaconate as secretary and DBC on the whole as clerk for many years. Her ministry in DBC dates to the early 1970s.

RESTARTING THE BOARD OF TRUSTEES

In DBC's earliest days, the church elected people to serve as "trustees" who would oversee certain financial and physical aspects of the church property. The last trustees from that first era (until 1983) were Jon Donner, Russell Viera, and Bob Whitlow. Then the use of trustees was suspended for a number of years as the church experimented with a "brethren model" single-leadership team. The need for trustee kind of help became evident again with a growing church. A "finance team" had been created by 1993, which included John Aanensen, David Hawkins, Judy Lemieux, Bonnie Furtado, Carol Bailey, and Barry Mingola. When the need became evident for a more comprehensive group of servants who were gifted for "trustee kind of work," the church agreed to reintroduce the election of trustees back into the life of DBC in October 1994. The new team included David Hawkins, John Aanensen, Mike Brown, Bruce Durfee (son of founding pastor Chaloner Durfee), Gina Mingola, and Frank Sinclair. This freed up the elders and diaconate to focus more clearly on their specific fields of ministry. A good and useful working relationship and balance has existed since then between the elders, the diaconate, and the trustees of DBC.

The trustees have developed many enhancements to the management and maintenance of DBC's assets. They provide ministries of oversight, planning, and service. One example is how the trustees have served DBC when the church more deliberately committed to a long-term plan to carefully comply with all major civil and fiscal parameters. These have come to be expected by the various governmental agencies as well as by the insurance industry. This is an ever-changing environment with changes of laws and the regular creation of new laws. We appreciate the good care of our trustees in being aware of these laws and learning of changes to law as they occur.

With the gradual decommissioning of the 1990s-era New Building Committee, our Trustees inherited the long-term completion of planned facility enhancements. They have sponsored many projects to our physical plant, its internal systems, improvement and continual upgrade plans for equipment, landscaping, work days, security and communications systems, and policy development. Eventually, a paid part-time maintenance facilitator is envisioned, as the Lord provides.

THE WOMEN'S SERVICE TEAM AND WOMEN'S MINISTRY TEAM

What began as the Women's Service Team in 1987 (with sixteen women) evolved into the Women's Ministry Team with a wider focus. Many women have served on this generalized ministry team over the years. Some of their planning oversight has focused on:

- The annual Christmas Party, which has met in various locations, including the old Abraham Manchester's Restaurant in Adamsville, White's of Westport, the old Sunset Room in the UMass Dartmouth Campus Center, the Salvation Army gym in New Bedford, and in our own facility. It is one of our few all-adult ministries and is loved by many.
- The Ladies' Tea, an annual event for women and friends in March of each year, with a guest speaker.

- Seminars, workshops, and small groups for women, with friendships flowing out of these events.

- Mentoring, which sometimes goes on more silently than out in the open. Some of our more mature Christian women find it on their hearts to pass on the lessons of Christian womanhood to younger believers, with much commitment and intentionality. It has been a deeply appreciated ministry of the Women's Ministry Team.

WINDOWS TO THE WORLD (2002)

Missions support came into DBC early but due to low finances was discontinued and then only sporadic for a time. In 1987 DBC began supporting David and Ruth Schaffer with Community Chaplain Service at $300 per year and added Kevin and Ping Whitehead, ministering with Operation Mobilization in Spain in the following year. Then what began somewhat tentatively in 2002 as a missions "group," then became strong and vibrant and very active in DBC. I imagined the title, and the idea was that in DBC there would be people who lead in looking out of our windows to the world for the gospel. Our view should be to look far (international missions), less far (national missions), and near (local missions). A balance of all three viewpoints for missions should be maintained, we have said.

The "Windows" group has sponsored missions conferences, missions projects, special one-time missions speakers, visits from the missionaries we financially support, the creation of a viable missions "policy" to govern how we support missions, and short-term missions trips. Recently our "Windows to the World" team has re-tooled the vision to see ourselves as ministering to *our* "Jerusalem, Samaria and to the uttermost ends of the earth." A new missions policy booklet was developed in 2012. Currently DBC supports eighteen missionary families or missions agencies, plus our own internal missions efforts at $55,000/year. We hope our missions program continues to grow and impact the outreach of DBC.

It took a long time to launch our own short-term missions trips. Two *aborted* missions trips are worthy of note:

- The Evangelical Alliance Mission (TEAM) missionary Tom Monk encouraged me to go on a short-term missions trip with him to Turnu-Severin, Romania, in 1992. Money was raised (mainly from Mullein Hill contributions, as I had spoken there many times), and I was ready to go, when at the last minute TEAM pulled out of Romania for security reasons. The funds were left with TEAM.

- In September 2004, Bob and Judy Pardon and I were going to lead a short-term trip to Beslan, Russia, with missionary (and long-time friend) Frank Carmical. However, when the Chechen rebels assaulted the school near there, Frank cancelled our trip, also for security reasons. The funds that had been raised to that point were saved and used for later missions trips.

Short-term missions trips successfully began, though, in the summer of 1992. DBC then commenced a long and blessed experience of sending our own people on short trips with a missions focus. The people going on the trips raised their support, prayer, and encouragement from others in DBC. After each trip, DBC received good, well thought-out, and well-presented reports. Trips to date for the past twenty years of DBC's history include the following:

- West Virginia: A youth missions trip under Assoc. Pastor Lou Parascand and youth leader Sylvia Morris, through *Group* ministries, summer 1992.
- Romania: Jocelyn Damgaard with Awana Clubs International, June 2000.

- Russia: Dominic Zarecki with Awana Clubs International, June 2001.
- Donner family missions trips, with Touch the World missions.
  - Rachel Donner to Livingston, Scotland, summer 2001.
  - Rachel and Debbie Donner to Livingston, Scotland, summer 2002.
  - Jon, Debbie, Sarah, Rachel, and Aaron Donner to Scotland, summer 2003.
  - Jon Donner to Livingston, Scotland, Debbie and Sarah to Ireland, Rachel to Romania, and Aaron to Germany, summer 2004.
  - Jon and Rachel to Livingston, Scotland; Aaron and Debbie to the Orkney Islands, summer 2005.
- Haiti: Pastor Neil with a team led by UMD Christian Fellowship president and The Master's Seminary (Los Angeles, California) student Willio Destin, including elder Larry Avila from Emmaus Christian Church and former UMD Christian Fellowship president (and DBC attender) Edwin Menon, August 2006.
- Aaron Donner to Papua New Guinea with New Tribes Mission. Rachel Donner to Victory Ministries' Camp Li-Wa, Fairbanks, Alaska (DBC missionaries Ron and Cheryl Gallegos minister there), summer 2007.
- Maine: Two youth missions trips to a Christian camp led by our Minister of Youth and Christian Education Tom Brown, 2007 and 2008.
- Tijuana, Mexico: Youth missions trip with Teen Mania's Global Expeditions attended by Leia Brunette, Steve Hawkins, and Bob Saunders, summer 2008.
- Trinidad: Leia Brunette went on a youth missions trip in 2009 with Teen Mania.

- Syracuse, New York: Youth missions trip to an inner city Rescue Mission led by our Youth and C.E. Associate, Natasha Ferro, 2010.
- Port-Au-Prince, Haiti: Susanna Damgaard with Samaritan's Purse, 2010.
- Albania: Michael and Lisa Gemaly with Spark Ministries, 2010.
- Flagstaff, Arizona: Youth mission trip to Indian Bible College, led by Youth and CE Associate Natasha Ferro, summer 2011. (DBC missionary Martha Gushee ministers there.)
- Fairbanks, Alaska- trip to Victory Ministries' Camp Li-Wa, where DBC missionaries (and former DBC members) Ron and Cheryl Gallegos minister, summer 2012. Trip leader was Sallie Wilson, accompanied by Shirley Barboza, Maria Latour, Cheryl Henlin, Rachel Donner, Michael Jacques, and Dillon Reinhard.

THE INCLUDERS AND THE HOSPITALITY TEAM

As DBC began to grow, it became evident that some focused effort was needed in enfolding visitors and new people. We wanted no one to be excluded or unnoticed. The first effort was a team called The Includers. This team lasted for a while and then ceased functioning. A revived effort commenced in 2007 with a good effort, and it was and is called the Hospitality Team. With this team there began a Sunday luncheon especially aimed at newcomers, though all are welcomed. The lunch is provided by a rotating team and is suspended at times when a break is needed. The Hospitality team also schedules greeters for both services, provides van rides from the UMD campus for students, and welcomed Janine Soldevilla in September 2011 as a part-time staff person to help with enfolding new people.

Men's Ministry Team

Ministries to men go all the way back in DBC history, but focused efforts really picked up steam with the Promise-Keepers movement in the mid-1990s. Two Promise-Keepers conferences in our own area were held (Middleboro and Taunton), and I helped with the early leadership of those events.

A men's ministry team was started in 2007, and they seek to minister to the unique needs of the men of DBC. Many conferences at Monadnock and elsewhere have been enjoyed, accountability groups offered, a special conference in 2011 in DBC, a Men's Sunday School class, a camera club, and other efforts to bring men together. Bob Whitlow has brought good leadership to this team, aided by Mark Ellis, Randy Desroches, Norm Dufault, Arthur Cadieux, and others.

Proverbs 3 College Outreach (2010)

A joint effort was started in 2010 to reach out to both U.Mass. Dartmouth students and our own children who have gone away to college elsewhere. It was the burden of elder Larry Logan and Youth and Christian Education Associate Natasha Ferro to maintain a meaningful connection with the students. Lynn Brown also assisted with the writing of cards and sending of "care" packages.

A new scholarship fund was also instituted in 2011 to provide assistance to our own students in their first year of college. Funds were designated from cash reserves, and two students were granted scholarships at the beginning of this ministry. This was elder Larry Logan's idea, and it was heartily approved by the elders and the body. An invitation is given to our own DBC high school seniors, who then fulfill a designated protocol to receive consideration for scholarship assistance for their first year of post-high school study or training.

Health Team (2010)

Debbie Donner, a registered nurse for many years, learned about "parish nursing" and took the training to become a "fellowship nurse" in DBC in 2010. The training was substantial, and she received a special Fellowship Nursing pin at its completion. Soon after she started a Health Team team in DBC to promote public health, give training opportunities to the body in various health-related matters, provide health screening, and develop a greater awareness of health around our church. She has been assisted by registered nurse Debbie Ashworth and others.

The University of Massachusetts at Dartmouth

Ground was broken for the new SMU campus in June of 1964. As mentioned, it was Pastor Chaloner Durfee's original thought that with a new university planned for construction in Dartmouth, there would be good opportunity for a new Baptist church to be planted and to grow along with the university, with intentional outreach to that community. Both Bill Jr. and Jim Hallett remember this being one of the things upon which Pastor Durfee had hoped DBC would focus. DBC's second pastor, James Harding, also was interested in reaching the university community, and some outreach was carried on from his pastorate through the pastorate of Mel Longtin (concluding in 1980). My burden for university ministry provided a renewed vision for what was possible, and even urgent, for DBC to explore. With a community of ten thousand people six hundred yards from DBC, it seems to me that it should be a priority to do all we can to make a good impact there. Many SMU/UMass Dartmouth students, faculty, and staff came through DBC over the years, and DBC has become known as a good home for UMass Dartmouth Christians.

A notable UMD faculty member, Dr. Dean Schmidlin, Professor of Electrical Engineering, first visited with me in my office in the fall of 1985. Dean and I struck up an immediate friendship, and Dean became a valued member of DBC. He was baptized along with several others in Turner Pond in July 1990. Dr. Schmidlin endeared himself as a gracious donator of DBC's first computer systems and served as a gifted Sunday School teacher, a competent counselor and friend, and finally as a longstanding (and much loved) elder in the church. He taught many innovative adult Sunday School courses and served as a financial counter and in many other capacities. His first class was a guided reading of Dr. Larry Crabb's *Finding God*, followed by a unique and thoroughly researched class on "A Christian Interpretation of Dreams." He continues to be a valued long-distance friend of DBC. Dean served as an elder from 1997 until his retirement from UMass Dartmouth and relocation to North Carolina in 2009.

Other UMass Dartmouth faculty members and research staff who also came into DBC for varying periods of time include Doctors Charlene Mello (and husband Christopher), Larry Logan (and wife Fran), Xiaoqin "Shelley" Zhang (and husband Liang Li), Maolin Guo (and wife Weiping Yang), John Fobanjong, Yu Zhou, and Shuowei Cai, Professor Robert Helgeland, research associate Dr. Hai-hong Wang, instructor Naa Akofio-Sowa, and PhD candidates Brad Harris (and wife Carrie), Ruiping "Mary" Ma, Tzuu-wang "Alex" Chang (and wife Jing Ping), and Emmanuel Agyei.

Over the years, not all DBC members have been moved with any need to place special focus on campus ministry. When I came in 1983, though the church was rebuilding itself, there was no interest in the university. However, over most of our history and in recent years, most in DBC have sensed a call to at least be alert to the unique opportunities for ministry provided by the church's proximity to the university. In the last ten years, many DBC members have reached out personally to UMD people. Most have seen the tangible good of ministry to students, faculty, and staff and the good reputation formed as these things unfolded over the years. How I would love to chat with Pastor Durfee about what he originally envisioned!

In 2007 I casually inquired about the possibility of acquiring a parking pass after unofficially ministering there for most of my twenty-four years in Dartmouth to that point. I had heard that multiple Protestant chaplains are recognized at the UMass Amherst campus and with that knowledge approached UMassD. Dartmouth Vice Chancellor for Student Affairs Dr. Susan Costa about possibly becoming an associate chaplain there. I was told that there was a protocol in place for such appointments, administered by her office and the Religious Resource Center on campus, led by Sister Madeleine Tacy, OP. Sister Madeleine was a well-known minister on campus who has served there since 1976.

I also learned that at that point there had been no Protestant chaplain on campus for three years, since the half-time Episcopal chaplain had been withdrawn from this campus due to "drying up" of denominational funding. Upon easily fulfilling the protocols, I gained appointment as sole Protestant chaplain, an unpaid volunteer and very part-time staff position. With no one representing a Protestant theology (let alone an evangelical perspective) on campus for several years and no one else seeking the position, the opportunity seemed like a clear open door from the Lord. I possessed the proximity, the academic credentials, the desire, and the on-campus support of Christians I knew there. The protocol includes current employment by a recognized religious institution, possession of at least a Master of Divinity degree, and demonstration of a sufficient community on campus who would desire the on-campus presence of a Protestant Chaplain. Vice Chancellor Costa, without ceremony, appointed me as Protestant Chaplain by letter in June 2007. It has been my privilege to be the second evangelical Protestant chaplain on this campus. Don Anderson (DBC's fourth pastor) briefly served there from 1973 to 1975.

Building Enhancements

Although caring for a building is not often thought of as a "ministry," its maintenance and improvement have gathered the spiritual gifts, effort, hard work, and creativity of a number of DBC people over the years. Working on our buildings and grounds can also serve as an "entry" effort for new people to take some ownership of our ministry in a practical way. Some of the projects that were completed (and fondly appreciated and remembered) include the following:

- **Bathroom renovations:** Mike Martin provided a renovation of the bathrooms in about 1978.
- **New exterior shingling**: Mike Martin re-shingled the building over its original exterior in 1978.
- **The "old kitchen" renovation**: Donald Rodriques donated new cabinetry in memory of his deceased mother about 1980.
- **The "Walls Project":** In an early 1990s project, Joe Tavares and Manny Pacheco undertook leadership of a major effort to redo all the upstairs interior walls, including a wonderful stenciling of the top of the walls by Sue Ponte and Joan Whitlow.
- Manny Pacheco and Paul Matson provided many shelving enhancements over several years (1990s).
- The "**Elevator Project:** Designed by architect Dan Lewis and constructed by Bob Graham and Lou Parascand (1993).
- The transition to **data projection** and *PowerPoint* (2001).
- Re-roofing, repainting, and residing the old building (2003).
- Addition of a new classroom in the old building by Bill Stack (2008).
- Sound and A/V enhancements overseen by Mathew Vangel (2010).

- Renovations on the old building (2009–11). The Trustees arranged for the installation into the old building of an interior French drain installation, sump pumps, a new floor, new insulation and walls, new doors and locks, new A/V connections and wiring, new furniture and A/V equipment, upgraded alarm system, and a drop ceiling added downstairs. The cost was approximately $30,000. Much volunteer labor and expertise was contributed by various members of the body and outside friends of DBC. Further renovations to the upstairs are anticipated for the near future.

Chapter 6

TRADITIONAL MINISTRY AND EVENTS

When I remember these things, I pour out my soul in
me: for I had gone with the multitude, I went with them
to the house of God, with the voice of joy and praise,
with a multitude that kept holyday. (Psalm 42:4)

Although DBC has explored many contemporary ways to
evangelize the lost, to disciple the saved, and to encourage
our people, we also joyfully engage the more traditional kinds of
ministry—all the typical events generally seen in churches.

BAPTISMS, WEDDINGS, FUNERALS

Many ceremonies of importance have been celebrated over the
years, many in the facility of DBC and at other locations. Baptisms,
weddings, rededication of marriage vows, dedications of Christian
families and children, ground-breakings and dedications of facilities,
funerals, and memorial services are some of the various kinds of
ceremonies that have been planned and carried out in DBC. While

downplayed by some, and with great variation of style, many members and staff of DBC have given time and attention in heartwarming dedication and affection in all of these events.

Some of the Baptized in the 1980s and 1990s: Dartmouth Bible Church practices the ordinance of believer's baptism—that is, the immersion of a person in water at his or her own request because of the personal desire to identify with Christ. DBC's original building included no baptistery tank and so other locations were found. In the '80s and '90s, the baptized under DBC's ministry included Debbie Halliwell, Dick Halliwell, Jennifer Rand, Marilyn Rand, Joe Tavares, Glenn Whitehead, Ron Tavares, Frank and Madeline Sinclair, Barbara Gahan, Dr. Dean Schmidlin (UMD), Gilly Pacheco, Kathy Mingola, Susan Blenkhorn, Christine Souza, Erik Aanensen, Linda Carreiro, Christine Ferguson, Donna Benard, Nanette LePage, Donna Riley, Paul and Shawn Matson, Ray and Donna Medeiros, Nancy Graham, Bob Graham, Matthew Whitlow, Jocelyn Damgaard, Susanna Damgaard, Tom Saunders, Candice LaBerge, Rita Cadieux, Dorothy Leung, Sarah Donner, Rachel Donner, Jeremy Corkum, Jason Corkum, John and Elizabeth Zarecki, Matthew Whitlow, Jeannette Souza, Rene and Lillian Bariteau, Diana Martins, Bruce Harrop, Will Ponte, Bill Leite, and Lisa Dennison. Locations included Onset Beach, Horseneck Beach, Turner Pond, Elim Baptist Church, Hope Evangelical Church, and various backyard swimming pools, notably at the home of Frank and Madeline Sinclair in Westport, who graciously hosted a number of summertime baptisms. (Appendix 4 lists the names of all baptized since 2000 to the present time.)

Underside of baptistery covers with names of the baptized recorded

New building: With the construction of the new building and installation of a fiberglass baptistery, we began a new tradition of recording the names of those baptized on the underside of the baptistery covers (see Appendix 4, listing the people baptized in DBC from February 2000 through January 2012.) Every baptism service has been a blessing, with many people attending. The worship team has provided music, and families of the church typically provide refreshments. Testimonies of how the Lord has worked are shared, and these services have been a source of much joy. I have often told people, "Come to our baptism—it's one of the best things we do!"

Weddings: It has also been a joy to celebrate weddings in DBC. I am unaware of any weddings performed in DBC before that of Victor and Shelly (Rogers) Boutin in 1984. After that there were Manny and Christine Souza, Gregg and Lisa (Montgomery) White, David and Vivian (Mingola) Hawkins (at First Nazarene), Paul and Christine (Depres) Souza (at First Nazarene), Ron and Susan (Blenkhorn) Brunette (on Chocoura Island, New Hampshire), Paul and Laura (Duarte) Crook, Joe and Cathy (Davis) Silva, Gary and Eileen (Platt) Herman; Matthew and Marlies (Aanensen) Hebert (at Fort Phoeniz, Fairhaven), William and Lisa (Teasdale) Leite (at Christian Fellowship Center, New Bedford), Francis and Lisa (Leite) Cote (by Rev. Louis Parascand), Mitchell and Rachel (Currier) Andrews (by David Schaffer), Gregg and Jennifer (Currier) Tavares, Matthew and Megan Whitlow, Matthew and Barbara (Zina) Cabral, Scott and Lois (Lackie) Messier, Dominic and Esther Zarecki (in Pasadena, California), Jonathan and Danielle (Methot) Marginson (at The Congregational Church of South Dartmouth), Jo-El and Elyse (Gonsalves) Kimaiyo, and Robert and Aubrey (Constant) Bruce (by Rev. William Stack).

Recommittal of Marriage Vows: An unusual service of Recommittal of Marriage Vows was held on June 6, 1999, for Steuart and Carol Bailey, David and Jennifer Cadieux, Paul and Laura Crook, Daniel and Susan DeAraujo, Tetsuro and Maki Oishi, Tom and Maureen Saunders, David and Ruth Schaffer, and John and Elizabeth Zarecki. Keith and Tatum Constant also recommitted themselves to their marital vows in DBC in 2001.

Funerals have been held in DBC for Nancy Graham, Frank Sinclair, Al Holmstrom, Rochelle Mingola, and Jose Sousa. A number of memorial services have been held as well.

Child Presentations/Parent Dedications have been held from time to time, although records have not been kept of the specific children dedicated by many couples. Child presentation/parent dedication is the step of Christian parents publicly dedicating themselves to raising their children under the sound teaching of the gospel and in the Christian faith.

A Dedication and Ground-breaking for the first building occurred in the fall of 1967 and a dedication of that building in June of 1968. Ground-breaking for the new building was held on December 9, 1998, and the Dedication in August of 2000. This service was attended by State Representative John Quinn, Northeast Baptist Conference District Executive Minister Paul Hubley, and DBC's second pastor, Jim Harding. Charter members William and Dorothy Hallett attended as guests, and music was provided by long-time DBC friend Dominick DeLuca and his band. A mortgage-burning ceremony was held in September of 2008.

Christian Education

Basic to evangelical Christianity is the idea of sharing and communicating the gospel and the Christian life to the next generation. DBC committed itself from the beginning to do everything possible to accomplish an effective ministry of Christian education to all children who could be reached, both within our own families and neighborhood and area children as well. Several ministries have supported this goal:

The Sunday School

Children's Sunday School Coordinators have included, among many, Judy Concepcion, Carol Bailey, Christine Souza, Elizabeth Zarecki, and Sallie Wilson.

Notable Sunday School teachers have been many, but Noelia Murphy deserves special mention. She has taught junior high Sunday School in DBC for many years and with much creativity, commitment to teaching the students the whole Word of God, and joy.

Multiple adult elective classes became the regular program in the early 2000s. Many good teachers brought classes, including Bill Hallett Jr., Donald Clapp, Dr. Larry Logan, Brendan Gahan, Dr. Dean Schmidlin, Valorie Schofield, Kathie Marginson, Mark Ellis, Bob Whitlow, and John Zarecki. Dean Schmidlin coordinated adult Sunday School for many years and himself developed a wonderful ministry as a teacher. His adult Sunday School ministry really "set the bar" for excellence in preparation, presentation, and spiritual direction.

Debbie Donner and I began co-teaching the senior high school class in 1994. In 2000 we transitioned to teaching eighteen- to thirty-year-olds, which we continue to do (2012). Sunday School has been a great blessing to us as we have watched the college-age members and beyond wrestle with many issues and grow in their faith.

CHILDREN'S CHURCH

A Children's Church was established at the time of the merger with Elim Baptist Church and has run with varying success over the years. Generally the program is offered as an alternative for children to the sermon. During the ministry of Tom Brown, it became especially successful, and that success has continued into the ministry of Natasha Ferro. Currently it is offered every Sunday during the second worship service.

THE NURSERIES

DBC's "nursery" ministries have depended on the good volunteer work of parents and older teens coordinated by long-term volunteer coordinators. For a time, a nursery was offered during both worship services but in later years has only been offered during the later service. Many have served over the years in the rarely appreciated work of being Nursery Coordinator. In recent years, Susana Thomas served DBC cheerfully and capably in this role.

PRAYER IN DARTMOUTH

All ministries of DBC have recognized the critical importance and privilege of prayer. In the early days of the church, prayer ministries were more formalized, with a Wednesday evening prayer meeting every week. Since 1980 or so, prayer ministries have been more varied and diverse. There have been many times of prayer, and every small group, class, team meeting, and service is both opened and closed in prayer. Prayer requests are shared often and repeatedly, with an expectation of God's answers to prayer and providence governing those answers. We pray for many outreaches and non-Christians as well, and we are always available to pray with people spontaneously and as needed. The elders pray for the sick and many other needs, and DBC people who are focused on missions remind us of the frequent needs for prayer on the mission field as well as the specific needs of our missionaries.

For several years, a week of prayer was engaged with nightly prayer meetings held in various homes. Prayer for special events is always encouraged, and no major decisions are made without a season of prayer and seeking the Lord.

PRAYER CHAIN

A prayer chain was started around 2000, with a good number of church members and attenders being available for immediate and even emergency prayer support. A prayer chain coordinator receives the initial request and passes it down the line to provide rapid prayer support to anyone who requests it. Nancy Graham began this ministry, and Rita Cadieux has coordinated our prayer chain in recent years.

PRAYER ROOMS

In 2010 a few in the church participated in the first prayer room ministry. Debbie Donner envisioned setting up a room in the church with several themed stations (i.e., worship, repentance, intercession, missions) and inviting people to sign up and pray in the room for an hour at a time. It would be a twenty-four-hour period of time with people praying in hour-long slots for personal revival, missions, the people of DBC, our country, and other subjects. By the winter of 2013, five such prayer room times have been held.

PRAYER SUPPORT BY E-MAIL

With the beginning of my weekly e-mail, *Meanderings,* in 2006, some prayer requests are forwarded to the bulk of the church body weekly. Also, prayer requests are regularly shared with the body through the Sunday bulletin, and prayer requests are also received via our church website.

Missions Prayer

A group of people have met regularly, off and on, for praying for our missionaries. This has been done at the church or hosted by various church members in their homes.

Worship in Dartmouth Bible Church

The goal of every church is to successfully worship God and to see His glory. Genuine worship blends good preparation by the participants with competent worship leadership, personal repentance, gratitude, authentic intent, and biblical truth. DBC has sought to value all of these over the years, although with varying success.

Dr. Duane Litfin (whose brother Roger candidated at DBC in September 1982) has written the following summary about worship, which I think is excellent:

> What is worship, after all? It's the act of acknowledging and praising God as God; indeed, as *our* God. It is the adoring response of grateful creatures to their Maker. In worship we come before God with awe and reverence, focusing on Him in loving contemplation, celebrating Him for who He is and what He has done. We willingly bow before Him in surrender, delighting in the privilege of extolling His worthiness. In worship we join our small voices with the celestial choirs in a grand chorus magnifying the Creator and declaring His excellencies: His purity, His power, His beauty, His grace, His mercy, His love.
>
> From the beginning, God has called His people to public worship. It's everywhere in the Bible, and with good reason: our corporate worship pleases God. What's more, we need it as well. Everyone who has ever built a campfire knows how quickly lone embers cool and die. But gather those embers and they create a furnace effect that burns hot. Corporate worship is designed to generate that furnace

effect in God's people. Those around us warm our spirits, encourage our faith, and hold us up when we're faltering. As Martin Luther famously put it, "At home, in my own house, there is no warmth or vigor in me, but in the church when the multitude is gathered together, a fire is kindled in my heart and it breaks its way through."

"Do not neglect the gathering of yourselves together," says the writer to the Hebrews (10:25). We come to faith as individuals, but Christ places us instantly into His body, and we require that body for the purposes of worship. There are aspects of worship we cannot fulfill alone. The Lord's Table, for example, belongs to the community; celebrate it when you "come together," says the apostle (1 Cor. 11:18, 33). So also baptism, corporate prayer, the public reading of Scripture, the teaching of Scripture, the corporate confession of sin: all these and more are designed for corporate worship.[23]

From its beginnings in the Durfees' living room until the early 1960s, worship was defined in DBC by a traditional Baptist order of service and sense of purpose. The elements were hymn-singing, offering, Scripture reading, pastoral prayers, teaching, and preaching. Changes occurred from that time until the construction of a new sanctuary, with the introduction praise choruses from *Maranatha! Music, Hosanna Music, the Vineyard Music Group, Hillsong,* and other contemporary sources, which came to largely replace the traditional hymns. The original hymnbooks were shelved in favor or *The Hymnal for Worship and Celebration*, published by Word Music in 1986, and its use for the opening hymn each week. The congregation is currently familiar with about three hundred hymns. The traditional Sunday evening and Wednesday evening services were abandoned after 1980 due to lack of interest and the

---

[23] http://www.christianitytoday.com/ct/2012/januaryweb-only/clothingmatters.html.

growing commitment to small groups ministry instead. For a time in the early 1980s, DBC experimented with the Plymouth Brethren practice of the open meeting, allowing for spontaneous teachings or exhortations by any male (and sometimes female) attendees. This was often problematic, and so the practice was later relegated to business meetings, coffeehouses, or other special events.

The Lord's Table was practiced in DBC from the beginning, traditionally on the first Sunday morning of each month, with the regular exhortation that only believers *should* participate, and the invitation is given frequently for the seekers to reach out in faith and to entrust themselves by faith to the Lord Jesus. Grape juice and bread squares are used. In 2008 the elders took the responsibility to be the servers and to dress with a more deliberate dignity.

With the construction of a larger and more elegant sanctuary, more possibilities opened up. Even the use of the word "sanctuary" seemed more real (to me, at least), as the space designed by architect Peter Brown deliberately reflected a sense of light and joy with lighter woods, many windows, and a prominent, vaulted front window design. At the same time, since this room was designed to be "multi-purpose" with an Awana circle laid into the carpet, movable chairs, tables, and doors, and using the room often for many purposes other than worship, the sense of "sacred space" is muted. This is evident especially in worship as our people are consistently jovial and conversational just before worship. However, on many quiet afternoons when the sun is just right, our sanctuary reflects the light and glows in a delightful reminder that we are recipients of *His* light in the gospel. Moving into a new facility precipitated a number of other interesting effects:

- The platform design by Peter Brown was both functional and visually appealing. It was designed for a worship team with many audio stations (provided by Bob Gordon of Stage Sound in Roanoke, Virginia) but retaining the traditional pulpit. The fiberglass baptistery was cleverly installed under the drum platform covers, which are removable and can be used as dressing room walls in each of the storage rooms on either side of the baptistery. It includes an automatic water feed and heating unit and drains by gravity out of the back of the sanctuary. An Awana circle was laid into the carpet and I suggested that the four colors be muted so as to be clearly distinguishable (red, blue, yellow and green) but more pastel-like. Another "sanctuary" detail known by few explains why there is an irregular angle to the top edges of the front windows. This gives the appearance of pointing upward, but it actually was an error in ordering by the contractor. At the time of delivery, with the discovery of the wrong-angled windows, DBC was offered the opportunity to retain the windows for installation in exchange for added dry-wall services by the contractor, which were not in the original "punch-list." We accepted this offer. In retrospect, the "flaw" actually replicates (quite by accident) a design feature used by the early twentieth-century New Bedford architect Peter Crapo!

- Offerings were traditionally received as part of the worship service until the early 1980s. At that time, a regular offering was discontinued and a box was provided at the rear of the little auditorium (another Plymouth Brethren–style practice). This was done until December 1999 when, with a new sanctuary, we decided to experiment once again with an offering as part of worship. There was reluctance by some to do this, but they were reassured that if it became distracting, we could always return to use of a box. We decided to try it for one year. To date we continue to use this approach with no unedifying effects. This also gave us the opportunity to utilize an "offertory" of special music or special readings provided by various people from the congregation. This has allowed the opportunity for people's gifts to be exercised in a more focused way. Also, I have made it my practice to find a fresh and specific item for which to give thanks each week. While my themes are probably predictable, I have always sought to make this my own gesture of worship and to share that with the body of believers as part of my role in worship leading.

- Projection of lyrics for songs, announcement graphics, video presentation, and the arrival of PowerPoint capability for sermon and ministry enhancement became a reality in October 2001, almost two years after we began worshipping in the new sanctuary. In that month we purchased, for $9,000 with services from Shanahan Sound, a Mitsubishi X400 (3,000 lumen) data projector with a special "long throw" lens. Networked to the sound booth computer, this capability greatly increased the variety of ways we could project video imagery. Bill Stack crafted the shelf and mounted the projector.

- The seating capacity is 225 adults, with use of overflow into the foyer. Normally, the seating is set at 180 chairs, which can be configured in any number of arrangements. Using movable chairs has facilitated a wonderful flexibility as changes are made for weddings and other occasional events. The coffeehouse ministry has been made possible by setting up tables and chairs. Also, we intentionally purchased comfortable chairs knowing we would be using them for many years—a lesson learned the hard way by many churches.

- The pulpit and communion table were retained from the first auditorium and nicely complemented the color scheme of the new wood in the sanctuary. With the merger with Elim Baptist Church in 1991, DBC inherited a wonderful Yamaha baby grand piano, a very serviceable organ, and

Elim's historic communion table. Elim had purchased an Allen organ (with a punched-card settings reader) and dedicated it to the Lord's worship in November 1971. For a number of years DBC "stored" the organ at the First Christian Church of Hixville, where it was used regularly. When we occupied our new sanctuary in 2000, we retrieved the organ and placed it there. However, since we rarely used it, we eventually made a gift of it back to the Hixville Church in 2005, where it is used to this day. The Elim/DBC piano was dedicated in 1978 in memory of Elim member Ethel Sturgis' father, Oscar Ekholm, of Elim's early days, and has served us well since. In the late 1990s, when I was speaking often at Mullein Hill Baptist Church in Lakeville, I noticed the very same organ and piano were being used in that church, a coincidental piece of *koinonia!*[24] Elim's original communion table was retained and is still used in the DBC church office as part of the secretary's center.

Major participants in the musical aspect of DBC's worship included in the earliest years Pastor Bill Stroup and Mr. William Hallett Sr., who played a small organ for hymn accompaniment for many years. (This organ was donated to Camp Clear in Carver, Massachusetts, in 1995, where it continues to be used to this day.) I myself also led worship from our arrival until a worship team was begun, occasionally joined by other guitarists and singers. Ron and Cheryl Gallegos brought much-needed talent and joy to worship while they were with us between 1988 and 1994. Then they were relocated to Missouri by Ron's employer. Cheryl was far and away the finest piano player DBC has had to date, and she also mentored and taught several young people how to play the piano while in our area. One fond memory I have was listening to Cheryl practice one

---

[24] "koinonia," κοινωνία, Greek for "fellowship" or the sharing of things in common.

day. I was particularly intrigued by the tune she was playing. It was a beautiful hymn called *Communion Hymn for Christmas* written by Margaret Clarkson and Tom Fetke, the editor of our hymnal. We introduced it at Christmas 1993 and have sung it regularly since, when communion is celebrated around Christmastime.

With a national trend among evangelical churches toward "blended worship" in the 1990s, we began our first "worship team" in 1995. Blended worship seeks to keep the good aspects of traditional music and add the refreshing aspects of the contemporary. This first worship team included Carol Bailey, Jonathan Donner, Elim pianist Emma Griffin, Paul Hsia, Ray Medeiros Sr., Regina Mingola, Donna Wingrove, and myself. Many others have shared in our worship team over the years, and this approach to leading worship has brought joy to many in our church and I believe has contributed to our numerical growth. Notable has been the ministry of professional and educational violinist, Susan Bouley, a faithful singing ministry for many years by Maureen Saunders, and other singers and instrumentalists, such as Ruth Schaffer, Hope Hallett, Dianne Ellis, Rita Cadieux, Tom Saunders, Doreen Clark, and David Cadieux. Recently our team has been joined by Nicole and Rebekah Bailey, who have both become regular pianists recently. Pianist Adele Nanfelt (wife of Rev. Ken Nanfelt) also has played for us on a number of occasions, with much appreciation. Adele is one of the finest Christian pianists I have ever heard and perhaps the best in southeastern Massachusetts.

Our current worship leader since 1994, Jonathan Donner, had also led worship earlier in the church's history in the early 1980s. With his return to us in 1994, DBC happily added Jonathan to our team and then to our paid staff (part-time) in 2005. In addition to good leadership, his love for worship, a keen and delicate sense of the presence of the Lord, as well as his musical abilities have always been plainly recognized and appreciated. Jon also composed a number of worship songs that have been appreciated by all and serve as a unique part of Dartmouth Bible Church's worship legacy. Occasionally he has been joined in singing by his wife, Debbie, and children, Sarah, Rachel, and Aaron. In recent years, Aaron Donner has been developing his own sense of song crafting and in addition to soloing has sometimes joined together with other younger singers, such as Alexander Zarecki, Robert Saunders, and Natasha Ferro.

Introducing drums to the worship ensemble of instruments was less controversial than I thought it might be. Our first drum set was a gift, via Mark Schaffer (David and Ruth's son), given to DBC by Max Weinberg's "drum tech," Harry McCarthy, the owner of Drum Paradise in Nashville. (Weinberg was music leader on *The Conan O'Brien Show,* television, and was in Bruce Springsteen's "E-Street Band.") DBC drummers have included Keith Constant Sr., Paul Crook, Dan Saunders, Amanda Murphy, and Ken Correia.

The current keyboard was donated by career professional accordionist Gene Demers, who attended DBC for a number of years and loved to play our Yamaha baby grand piano (from Elim) but only with no one present in the building! Gene did not play piano for DBC worship, feeling strongly that as a career accordionist, he could not competently play piano. This was to my deep regret, because I always felt he could play magnificently. Such are the ironies of church life!

Worship in Dartmouth Bible Church can be characterized as lighthearted and informal, yet dignified and orderly, with a strong focus on the exposition of Scripture and a heartfelt attempt to use meaningful music. From the merger with Elim in 1991 until construction of the new building in 1999, DBC had two worship services separated by Sunday School. In those years, DBC went back to one service for July and August of each year but continued Sunday School for the summer. With use of the new sanctuary, we held a single worship service until growth again enabled us to offer two services, beginning in 2004. Our general order of worship (averaging seventy-five minutes since 2004) is as follows:

- Early prayer time open to anyone, in the pastor's office
- ⋅ Welcome and announcements
- An opening hymn, with lyrics projected and hymnbooks made available
- Opening prayer
- Worship song set, with three to five contemporary songs and choruses
  - ○ In recent years, some contemporized hymns have regained inclusion into the "song set"
- Offering comments and prayer with ushers
- Scripture reading, related to the sermon
- Sermon
- Closing song
- Closing prayer

CONFERENCES AND RETREATS

Bible Conferences

The concept of "Bible Conferences" goes back to the end of the nineteenth century and saw a great growth in popularity across the United States and England in the 1920s. I had experienced many good Bible conferences in the churches of which I was part as a young Christian and always wanted to bring the practice to DBC. Here is a list of the speakers DBC has hosted under my ministry, to date:

1986—Dr. Donald Sunukjian, Th.D., Ph.D. Professor of Pastoral Ministries at Dallas Theological Seminary – a Bible Conference weekend focusing on the Book of Esther. This was DBC's first real Bible conference.

1987—Mr. Fred Funches, New England–area representative for The Navigators. I had known Fred from a distance in Virginia when I had first become a Christian in 1972.

1987—Dr. Roger Nicole, Professor of Theology at Gordon-Conwell Theological Seminary– only eight people attended this one-evening presentation. Dr. Nicole was very gracious though and brought the eight of us a fresh update, just having attended the International Council on Biblical Inerrancy before driving down to DBC from South Hamilton.

1988   My own mentor, Dr. Jack Arnold (Th.D.) brought a busy weekend Bible conference. Jack had himself been mentored by Dr. S. Lewis Johnson who in turn, had been mentored by Dr. Donald Grey Barnhouse.

1994   Dr. John D. Hannah, Professor of Historical Theology at Dallas Theological Seminary, brought a great weekend Bible Conference in April of that year, just after my own father had passed away. Dr. Hannah was very comforting to me and had been a favorite professor of mine at DTS. As I picked him up at Yale, where he had been doing a post-doctoral year of study in the writings of Jonathan Edwards, Dr. Hannah handed me a little piece of paper with tiny writing on it. He asked me, "Do you know what you're holding?" It was the original little manuscript for *Sinners in the Hands of an Angry God*. Dr. Hannah has recently published a wonderful history of Dallas Theological Seminary entitled *An Uncommon Union: Dallas Theological Seminary and American Evangelicalism* (2009).

2004, 2005, 2006—Dr. Ronald Blue, Professor of Missions at Dallas Theological Seminary, brought weekend Bible conferences to DBC in the springs of 2004, 2005, and 2006. He was much loved and appreciated in our church.

Mr. Frank Carmical—a longtime friend of Pastor Neil and fellow student at Dallas Seminary, Frank worked for years with "4-14," a cooperative ministry to Awana Clubs International, and with his own evangelistic and church planting ministry called Harvester Ministries travelling to many countries of the world. He spoke in DBC many times and we enjoyed his energy, enthusiasm and creativity very much. His current ministry is called Preaching Friend, in which he plans to assist many churches in many countries via an Internet training program for preaching God's Word. Frank was the featured speaker in three missions conferences and has visited and spoken in DBC *eleven* times since 1991. DBC has financially supported Frank since 2004.

2010 (October)—Rev. Randy Pizzino of Roanoke, Virginia, a good friend of mine, brought a weekend Bible conference and men's ministry focus in October 2010. Randy now ministers with Equipping Pastors International, Inc., and travels to Uganda, Rwanda, and Kenya to minister to pastors there. He and I shared a year on the same pastoral staff in Virginia in 1978. He is one of the finest preachers I have ever heard.

2011 (May)—Mr. Dwight Knight, from Detroit, Michigan, was brought to DBC by the men's ministry for a weekend family and marriage conference.

2011 (July)—Dr. Jimmy DeYoung, from Chattanooga, Tennessee, and a world-class scholar on the subject of Israel in prophecy, brought a mid-week prophecy conference in July 2011. This was the best generally attended conference in the history of DBC, with a full sanctuary every night (although only about sixty DBC people attended). DeYoung's wide appeal brought out many to hear him speak.

2012 (November)—Local pastors Jon Helm (First Church of the Nazarene in New Bedford), John Lloyd (Christ Community

Church in East Taunton), and Kory Tedrick (Mullein Hill Baptist Church in Lakeville) brought a series of messages focusing on the Ten Commandments. On this occasion also, I brought in a worship team made up of present and former UMass Dartmouth Christian Fellowship members who provided a wonderful song service, including four Presidents of the Fellowship.

Missions Conferences

DBC sponsored several missions conferences since the 2000s. The purpose was to increase missions awareness within DBC and offer a platform from which our own missionaries (and new ones with whom we were as yet unacquainted) could share the stories of the mission to which they were called.

Marriage Weekends

This began in the early 2000s when DBC began to connect with Family Life Today ministries. Their regional conferences, called *A Weekend to Remember*, are a national network of yearly marriage weekends held at prominent hotels. It was an attraction to us, and a number of DBC couples attended, some multiple times. In 2012 DBC hosted our first "Love and Respect" weekend, with video speakers Dr. Emerson and Sarah Eggerichs. Our video conference was attended by seventy people and was deemed a success. Our desire has been to provide whatever resources would be of genuine help to our couples and would be accessible and affordable. We also hosted Dr. and Mrs. Dan Verrengia for a Valentine's weekend in 1998. Dr. Verrengia was a counselor and at that time an elder at Grace Chapel in Lexington. He is now the Minister of Pastoral Care at Park Street Church in Boston.

DBC people also have enjoyed attending many conferences, retreats and seminars in other places. These have included the following.

NEACE

During the 1990s, the Evangelistic Association of New England (later called Vision New England) sponsored and operated a yearly Christian education conference called the New England Association of Christian Education (NEACE) conference. This was held in various large churches, and DBC people attended for a number of years. The conference featured significant speakers in the area of Christian education, many useful workshops, and a large exposition and resource fair. Those of us who attended always enjoyed the day and the fellowship.

ELDERS' RETREATS

The elders of DBC held three retreats together to pray, plan, discuss, and envision how the Lord wanted DBC to grow. These retreats began on a Friday night and lasted through Saturday. They were held at the Viking Hotel in Newport in 1998, at the Iyanough Hills Hampton Inn in Yarmouthport in 1999, and on campus at UMass Dartmouth in 2006.

DBC CAMPING TRIPS

At least twice the DBC family spent a weekend together camping, once at Bourne State Park (just after Renée and I arrived in 1983) and at Rumney Bible Conference with Dr. Howard Hendricks speaking in 1997.

CONGRESS (1990–2005)

People from DBC always looked forward to the large, interdenominational Christian conference held in Boston each winter called "Congress," sponsored by Vision New England. Attended by at peak ten thousand Christians, this conference featured some of the most well-known evangelical speakers and teachers in the nation, excellent music, and many resources in the exposition area of the Hynes Auditorium. I always looked forward to seeing Christians with whom I was acquainted from all over New England. Due to financial pressures, "Congress" was discontinued after the 2005 conference.

Men's and Women's Conferences

Promise-Keepers and Iron Sharpens Iron conferences received much appreciation from DBC men who attended. Also, the Monadnock Retreat Center's Men's Retreats (in New Hampshire) have been attended by DBC men and enjoyed greatly. This has been a great opportunity for men to get to know each other and develop some bonds between them. DBC women have attended and enjoyed Women of Faith and Monadnock Retreat Center Women's Retreats for a number of years beginning in the mid-1990s.

SoulFest

The SoulFest event is a large Christian music and teaching festival in Gunstock, New Hampshire, and DBC teens and college age members as well as some adults began attending in 2008. SoulFest provided camping, fellowship, music and discipleship opportunities for all who attended.

The Libraries

Every established church, it seems, has a library because Christians tend to be "readers" and DBC has been no exception. Upon my arrival at DBC in 1983, the church had a library of leftover books from previous pastors. I have always loved books, so I immediately took it upon myself to weed through that collection, merge a few books with my own library, and reconfigure the remainder into a new, usable collection for the body of DBC. When DBC merged with Elim Baptist Church in 1991, we inherited Elim's large library. Most of its holdings were dated, but through a joint effort in 1993 between myself and Cheryl Gallegos and Carol Bailey, we sorted through the approximately one thousand volumes from Elim and enfolded the usable volumes into the DBC library.

With the creation of DIBS in 2002, it was my thought to begin a permanent collection of quality Christian books, which we would call "the Research Library." This non-circulating collection is held in the old pastor's office/conference room in the original building and now includes about five hundred volumes. However, with the shift to electronic storage and archiving of books, it remains to be seen how this will affect church libraries over time. We have also experimented with providing a computer with *Logos* Bible study software, which is potentially an excellent resource but challenging to use.

DBC also maintains a main circulating library of about five hundred books, video and audio teachings, and several "collectibles." On the wall of that library are hanging a page from a vellum fifteenth-century Coptic Bible, a page of an original 1608 Geneva Bible (the version used by the Pilgrims), a page of a seventeenth-century Hebrew Bible, and a very special wall hanging given to us by a missionary to China. This "batik" was created in Kunming province of China by very poor Christians and depicts several scenes from biblical history. I wonder about what will become of my personal library in time. It is also a theological and exegetical collection, and I pray that the Lord will eventually lead me to a good home for it, and to keep it intact. It contains some fifteen hundred quality theological and biblical works.

TECHNOLOGICAL ADVANCEMENTS

DBC has kept pace with the flow of technology, and we have explored every way to enhance our ministry with it. This has included a transition from hymnbooks to physical overhead projection to

PowerPoint and Mediashout software via a data projector. When we were getting ready to move into the new building in late 1999, two friends of mine from the 1970s travelled to Dartmouth from Roanoke, Virginia, to provide the installation services for sound in the new sanctuary. Bob Gordon and Larry Arrington came at their own expense and spent several days installing, calibrating, and testing the sound system. Bob Gordon even donated a new *Allen & Heath* sound-mixing board, and while DBC paid for all the other new equipment, Bob's and Larry's considerable services were donated. This was a significant gift to our church and demonstrated once again the connection and kinship between believers in the Lord Jesus Christ.

More recently Mathew Vangel has come alongside DBC and donated many hours and much equipment to help DBC keep pace with audio/visual developments. He has been a real blessing to us. Three additional data projectors have been installed in various classrooms. DBC's computer network has grown significantly as well, enabling a more efficient ministry with all that a good network provides. From the original "PC" donated by Dr. Schmidlin in 1986, DBC now possesses six networked computers, a wireless network, and a large Konica network printer/copier/scanner. Much thanks to David Hawkins, his son, Bill Hawkins, and others who are constantly helping us improve our systems.

Our first website was created by Christopher Anderson in 1998, followed by a new design by UMass Dartmouth graduate student, David Chung in 2003 (his final MBA project). Another new design was provided by UMass Dartmouth digital media student Jonathan Marginson in 2005, and finally yet another design by Worcester Polytechnic Institute computer science student Bill Hawkins in 2010. Since the year 2000, the church website has been found to be the most fruitful means of attracting visitors and relocated Christians to DBC.

OUR CHINESE MINISTRY
(1996 TO THE PRESENT)

Early in my ministry, opportunities arose to befriend Chinese members of the SMU and U Mass Dartmouth community. In the early 1990s, the Chinese Student Association requested use of our building for occasional activities, and we happily hosted Chinese New Year and other events. I also met the occasional graduate student or freshman faculty member, who I felt I could help in one way or another. This included Dr. Hong Liu (later Professor of Electrical and Computer Engineering) and SMAST Fisheries and Oceanographic Research Associate Dr. June (Yue) Jiao and others. In 2005 I was invited to attend the ongoing Chinese Bible study on campus and met other Christians or "seekers" from the campus Chinese community, notably Dr. Shuowei Cai, Dr. Maolin Guo (and his wife, Weiping Yang), Dr. Tim Su, and Dr. Xiaoqin "Shelley" Zhang. I greatly enjoyed attending this study, and eventually it merged with a general faculty and staff Bible study.

I came to join David and Ruth Schaffer in their love for the Chinese community locally and gradually decided that I would focus my Doctor of Ministry dissertation on a topic that may prove helpful to that community. It was entitled *A Case Study of Three Evangelical Chinese Language–Based Churches in Southern New England,* and it studied churches in Acton, Amherst, and Worcester, Massachusetts, with a view toward laying groundwork for a possible Chinese church in Bristol County.

David and Ruth Schaffer have provided a weekly English-as-a-Second-Language ("ESL") class in DBC since 1996, which has also welcomed people from Japan, Vietnam, and occasionally from other countries. Currently a Chinese Bible study meets concurrently with the mid-week DBC Awana program, and a number of Chinese-American children have happily become a meaningful part of the

Awana program. A Chinese language library of good Christian books has also been started.

DBC 101, ETC.

The concept of church membership receives varying reaction. For some it is a natural step; after attending for a while, they see joining the church as a normal and positive step. Others view it with skepticism and suspicion. Negative past experiences, concern for personal autonomy, or just reluctance to make commitments has kept many from joining DBC. In 2006 the elders came across the books *The Purpose Driven Life* and *The Purpose Driven Church* by Southern Baptist pastor Rick Warren from Saddleback Church in Lake Forest, California.

Based on Warren's book *The Purpose Driven Church*, the elders developed a DBC strategy for membership, the first seminar of which is called "DBC 101." This includes a thorough introduction to all of the major aspects of what life in DBC includes, our attitudes, priorities and history. All membership candidates go through a standardized course workbook (compiled by Dr. Dean Schmidlin), and eventually the elders intend to develop follow-up seminars entitled "DBC 201" (How to Mature in the Christian Life), "DBC 301" (How to Find Your Personal Ministry), and "DBC 401," (How to Connect with Mission). The intent is to encourage the entire membership to take all of the follow-up seminars.

Membership records have been kept since the beginning of DBC's history, and the church has seen several hundred people as members at one time or another. Currently DBC has 113 active members.

DARTMOUTH BIBLE CHURCH'S PROGRAM TO HELP YOU GROW
BASIC CHRISTIAN LIFE AND SERVICE SEMINARS

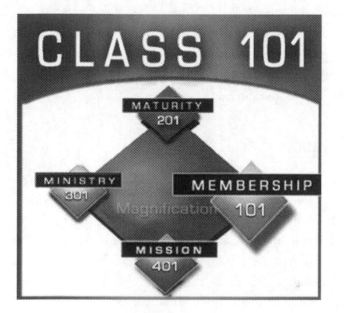

GO ON TO SECOND BASE!

AN OVERVIEW OF THE SEMINARS

TWENTIES (2008–PRESENT)

In 2008 a group of "twenty-somethings" in DBC began to meet weekly for fellowship, Bible study, prayer, and social activities. UMD graduate student Glenn Chamberlain led the group, which met usually in a local restaurant. The group desired participants from other like-minded churches, and several people from other churches did attend. The group remained small, and upon Glenn's graduation and relocation, leadership passed to a new group including Aaron Donner and Megan Pacheco (UMD grad and former Christian Fellowship president and Lighthouse Assembly of God attender). The group grew, and in early 2011, it merged with the "twenties" group from the First Church of the Nazarene in New Bedford. By late 2011, the group had grown to about fifteen regular participants and renamed themselves "Upper Room." In 2012 the group has grown to twenty-five people and has now renamed themselves "Strive."

DIBS (2002–2009)

I was always impressed with the little "biblical institute" I experienced in Roanoke, Virginia, in the late 1970s, which was called The Roanoke Institute of Biblical Studies (R.I.B.S.) I took several classes there under my mentor, Dr. Jack Arnold. In Dallas, during my fourth year at the seminary, I taught a semester in the Dallas Theological Seminary *Lay Institute* and enjoyed it greatly. The course I taught was called "How to Make Disciples" and ran in the fall of 1982. Years later, in Dartmouth, I sensed the need for a college-level instructional program in Bible and theology for the South Coast, Massachusetts, area, which would not be limited to DBC people or controlled by any expectation that attendees should necessarily attend DBC. What exists in abundance in other places in the country was almost unheard of here.

An experimental ministry—the Dartmouth Institute of Biblical Studies (DIBS)—began in 2002 and concluded in 2009. One hundred twenty-two people took courses, offered by eleven faculty members who all possessed at least a master of arts degree. Three possessed an earned doctorate, and four others possessed a Master of Divinity or Master of Theology degree. As part of DIBS, the entire program known as "The Theology Program" was used as was "The Truth Project," both of which were greatly appreciated by the students who took those DIBS courses. Others caught this vision and we had excellent instructors who donated time, effort, and heart for the Word of God and a solid evangelical theology. Those instructors included:

- Dr. Greg Gifford (MDiv, DMin) had the vision with me in the beginning, before he relocated to Ohio.
- Dr. Beryl Barkman (PhD). As a retired university professor, Dr. Barkman taught two semesters of Old Testament Introduction before relocating to North Carolina.
- Rev. Robert Pardon (MDiv, ThM) is a close friend and was with us for the whole seven years. He was a warm, thorough, and patient instructor with a wonderful background and ministry as director of the New England Institute for Religious Research. Bob was my right-hand man in DIBS.
- Rev. Bill Stack (MDiv) has a great love for the Word and for teaching it. He taught several courses in DIBS and continues as an elder in DBC.
- Rev. David Schaffer (STB, MDiv) taught a couple of courses early in DIBS. His maturity in Christ and love for the Word were very evident to his students.
- Rev. Roger Allen (MDiv) was a pastor from Middleboro with a unique musical gift. He taught one course on "The Psalms and Music" before relocating to Virginia.
- Mr. Mark Conrad (MS) was a retired US Navy officer and had a good take on leadership in the church. He brought a collaborative class on leadership, utilizing several guest speakers.
- Mr. Richard Setteducati (MEd, MS) was one of our own members and a retired high school science teacher. He brought a course on creationism and science. He then relocated to North Carolina, very near where his good friend from DBC, Dr. Dean Schmidlin, now lives.

- Mr. Ken Harman (BA, ThB). One of my closest friends, Ken offered a course in the doctrine of the church before relocating to North Carolina (coincidentally, the same town to which Dr. Beryl Barkman relocated).
- Mr. Brendan Gahan (MA). Another DBC leader, Brendan taught a course in Galatians.
- Rev. Dr. Neil Damgaard (ThM, DMin) taught courses in thirteen of fourteen DIBS semesters and directed the institute.

I received faithful administrative support from Mary Anne Dufault and Valorie Schofield, and a number of women also served as "hostesses," providing refreshments for the break time on DIBS nights. Financially, I asked all students for a donation as part of registration and used that money almost entirely for stipend-type gifts for each faculty and support member at semester's end. I took no stipends for myself but did purchase one data projector for the institute out of the proceeds. When DIBS ended, the remaining small balance of funds was given to DBC. Personally, I learned many lessons through creating and operating DIBS and through teaching the courses I offered.

Additionally, eleven individuals began attending DBC at least for a period of time as a result of first taking DIBS classes, and we first met current staff-person Janine Soldevilla and her husband, Brian, through DIBS.

Staff History

As a church grows, so do its needs for focused and compensated ministry people. DBC has been blessed with the services and ministries of a number of people over the years as it has grown from very small church, to small church, to a small to mid-sized church. Each staff person over the years contributed his or her own "fingerprint" on our ministry and blessed our church, contributing to its growth in various ways. Summarizing again, here are the pastors who have served DBC:

1. Rev. Chaloner Durfee (1963–64)
2. Rev. Jim Harding (1965–69)
3. Rev. Ray Leavitt, interim (1970–73)
4. Rev. Don Anderson (1973–75)
5. Rev. William Stroup, interim (1975–76), eight months
6. Rev. Mel Longtin (1976–80)
7. Rev. John Fernandez, interim (1981), six months
8. Rev. Dr. Neil Damgaard (May 1983–present)
    a. Associate Pastor Rev. Louis J. Parascand Jr. (Jan. 1991–Oct. 1993)

In addition to the pastors, the following people have served DBC in variously compensated roles:

- Mary Sylvia, secretary (1979–1980)
- Linda Matson, janitor (1982–1992)
- Guy Lumpkin, pastoral intern from Dallas Seminary (1987)
- Sylvia Morris, janitor (1992–2000)
- Paul Souza, youth pastor (2001–2005), full-time
- Glenn Grenier, janitor (2000–2005)
- Tom Brown, Minister of Youth and Christian Education (2006–2009), full-time
- Judy Lemieux, janitor (2005–present)
- Lynn Brown, secretary (2001–present)
- Jonathan Donner, Worship Leader (2005–present)
- Natasha Ferro, Youth and Christian Education Associate (2009 – present.) Promoted to Director in November 2012, full-time.
- Janine Soldevilla, Enfolding Leader (2011–present)

In recent years, both the leadership and the membership of DBC have been very open to the idea of expanding our staff as needs for doing so present themselves and resources (finance and space) make it possible. We seek to trust the Lord to show us how He is leading in this important area of church growth and to provide us with the wisdom and resources to capably manage an expanding staff. In 2010, through a collaborative effort between the Elders and Trustees, DBC's first employee handbook was created and implemented. This document is intended to provide a baseline from which standardized employee benefits and policies can be communicated and managed for the best interest of all who work for our church and in a Spirit-filled way. It is hoped that we always treat our staff with great fairness and a plentitude of generosity.

My Own Ministry— Rev. Dr. Neil Damgaard

Summarizing one's own ministry can be tricky, but here are a number of high moments from my ministry at DBC, from my own perspective:

1. Stabilization of Leadership and Growth in Membership. At Dartmouth Bible Church, we have established a multi-board and multi-team ministry that runs the church and sustains all aspects of our work, delicately balancing power and influence in our church. I have come to believe that power and influence are infrequently acknowledged realities in many organizations (especially in churches). Ironically, all too often it is *especially* churches that carefully protect and monitor power and influence, even while it is felt to be unspiritual to talk about these factors. In our church we have sought to understand the mind of Christ in creating, sharing, and accommodating

power and influence. Official boards include the Elders, the Diaconate, and the board of Trustees, which was preceded by a Finance Team. In addition to these boards, a growing staff has developed and this is has become the fourth "leg of the table" of leadership. We recovered older ideas which as it turned out made a lot of sense after all.

2. THE DEVELOPMENT OF MANY NEW TEAMS. A number of good teams have been established. They include Awana Clubs, Christian education, a coffee house team, worship, missions (which we call "Windows to the World,") Women's and Men's Ministries teams, Mothers of Pre-Schoolers (MOPS), a Hospitality team, a Health team, and a team of Youth leaders. Currently, a new staff "personnel" team and a security team are anticipated in 2013. My belief is that ministry- sharing, training, and a feeling of ownership of the church's ministry are best served by a team approach.

3. VISITATION IS CONSTANT AND ALWAYS INTERESTING. From the beginning of my ministry until now, I have engaged a regular and vigorous schedule of visiting members and attendees of DBC. Whether they are in-home visits, evangelistic one-on-one visits, meeting with DBC people at their place of employment, visitation in the hospital for many reasons or in nursing homes, in funeral parlors, remote wedding locations, or visiting at a local restaurant or diner just for coffee, visitation has been a joy and a regular part of every ministry week.

4. EXPLORATION OF EXPANSION POSSIBILITIES with Christian builder and Central Baptist Church (Middleboro) member A. P. Whitaker from 1987 to 1990. Although it was a testimony to the Lord, as stated early in this book, the little building to which Renée and I came was very small.

Any growth at all would quickly put DBC in a space crisis. Whitaker had completed many church projects in southern Massachusetts, including the addition to the First Christian Church of Hixville, the ministry building at Central Baptist Church in Middleboro, Mullein Hill Baptist Church in Lakeville, Pocasset Baptist Church in Pocasset, and many others. Although Al Whitaker did not end up being the contractor we used to construct our second building, he showed us possibilities and instilled a positive and possibility perspective. He gave us a confidence we needed at the time.

5. BEGINNING OF A PRESENCE WITHIN THE SMU (LATER UMASS DARTMOUTH) COMMUNITY. It has been my own vision to see DBC become a place the university community would both notice and appreciate. My goal for this is to create a base from which the gospel itself can be introduced and supported in the university environment. Enhancing this goal is the strategy to provide any community service or blessing that we can provide the university. We are always looking for ways to let 285 Old Westport Road know that 52 Morton Avenue is just down the street and is standing by as a valued friend, even as we desire to be viewed in the same ways by the Town of Dartmouth itself. At SMU my first contacts in 1983 were students James Gomes (who became a DBC member for a season), Greg Chopoorian, Melissa Oliver, and Campus Crusade staffer (from Brown University) Kent Dahlberg. DBC welcomed many students over the years, and a few became a part of our church, notably David Hawkins and Susan (Blenkhorn) Brunette. Later faculty, graduate students, staff, and international students would find their way to DBC.

6. BEFRIENDING MANY AREA EVANGELICAL FELLOW MINISTERS AND PASTORS and seeking connection and unity within the evangelical community in the area. It is almost a regional characteristic for most evangelical churches in the area to be isolated from each other and to hardly notice each other. For me this has always seemed a huge contradiction to our claims to love the New Testament. It has been my endeavor to establish and support meaningful and helpful connections between us without calling anyone to compromise their distinctions. Several small and fiercely independent churches have not responded to my overtures but a number of other churches and ministries have done so. To date, since 1983 I have come to know and appreciate over fifty area pastors. They are a great and precious resource to the cause of Christ in southeastern Massachusetts. If I have learned one lesson from all of them, it is their (and my) need for prayer, more prayer, and frequent prayer by their own flocks and by as many others as can be found.

7. MERGER WITH ELIM BAPTIST CHURCH IN APRIL 1991. This was essentially a two-year process that netted blessings for all who remained with the newly merged ministry. Many friendships were established, and Elim's assets made possible the construction—along with much additional sacrificial giving by church members—of the new facility in 1999, after an eight-year wait. Enfolding all the church members into a single integrated church family took longer than two years, as old loyalties are not shed easily. The merger experienced some losses of both Elim and Dartmouth members who simply could not tolerate a new kind of "family." The merger was one of the greatest challenges for me personally, and it was a time of really

trusting the Lord to lead, provide, and transform character to make us willing to accept change and excitement about advancing the ministry of the gospel.

8. REAFFILIATION WITH THE BAPTIST GENERAL CONFERENCE IN 1994. This was not an earth-shattering change for day-to-day operations for our church, but it was a healthy move. In the beginning the affiliation provided a health-insurance option for the pastors, though the Conference discontinued this offering soon after we merged. We have happily supported BGC (now *Converge*) ministries since that year, primarily through support of BGC missions and my own service as a district Trustee for six years. For myself, I appreciated the opportunity to learn how to participate in a larger affiliation, which was a new experience for me. I was glad to serve in the district too, and I continue to feel that reaffiliation was an important step for DBC.

9. COMPLETION OF THE NEW CONSTITUTION AND BY-LAWS. From the church's beginning, the Constitution and By-Laws document had been an evolving work. Mike Martin observed (1985 DBC Annual Report):

In 1976 Mel Longtin formed a committee to study the Constitution and By-Laws. His desire was to see that the church was governed by a document that had withstood the test of biblical study. The existing Statement of Faith and [basic] Constitution and By-Laws had been taken from the old Baptist General Conference and in many ways were felt to be effective for a rebuilding Dartmouth Baptist Church. Pastor Longtin and the Constitution and By-Laws Committee, worked hard primarily on the Statement of Faith—the basic foundation to the direction that the Dartmouth Baptist Church would take in 1981 ...

When we came in mid-1983, I immersed myself in the process too. Many changes and new versions have been voted into place over the years, and many hours have been devoted to improving this foundational document of the church. It took years to finalize that version, and the most recent revision is dated February 8, 2004. The Church Covenant is read together as part of each Annual Congregational Meeting. The Affirmation of Faith is carefully taught as part of each membership class, as are the operational portions of the Constitution and the By Laws.

10. ORDINATION OF THE FIRST GROUP OF MEN TO WORK TOGETHER AS ELDERS. In the early 1980s, Mike Martin and Tom DeCosta served briefly as church elders. Much later, though, Brendan Gahan, Dean Schmidlin, Frank Sinclair, and Robert Whitlow were ordained to be elders in 1997. In the years before, only Bob Whitlow and myself were considered elders. Thus we created a temporary office which we called "elder-advisor", which included several men and the women mentioned earlier in this book. Fifteen men have served as elders thus far in the history of the church (see Appendix 2). Finding men called for this ministry is done carefully and with a minimum of a two-year training period. DBC has been blessed by good elders in its first five decades, and we hope to always have an adequate board of elders. We are always on the lookout for servants with a heart for shepherding, teaching sound doctrine, and being a blessing to the church body.

11. DESIGN AND CONSTRUCTION OF A NEW FACILITY IN 1998 AND 1999. Credit should first be given first to God, who provided and sustained this giant effort. Made possible by the merger with Elim (the idea of which was conceived

first by former DBC Associate Pastor and former Elim Pastor Lou Parascand) the new building has proved a great enhancement and attraction for new church members. Currently, every inch of the facility is fully used and appreciated. While it took years to recover my stamina and energy for new projects, I laughingly tell people today that I have another building inside of me! With its completion in 2000–2001, the feeling of satisfaction and excitement drove me to give thanks to the Lord for all He had done for us.

12. PROMOTION AND SUPPORT OF SMALL GROUPS MINISTRIES. Since about 1980 small groups have been an important and deliberate part of DBC. While small groups *can* distract people's attention from, and appreciation for the overall body life of a church, their benefits far outweigh their potential problems. As of 2012, DBC has about fifteen small groups. Of special note has been the great gift of hospitality and joy for small groups from Bob and Joan Whitlow, who have led small groups in their home and elsewhere for over thirty years.

13. ADDITION OF STAFF WORKERS. The leading of the Lord and the people's willingness to find and fund staff workers has made it possible to utilize on a professional level the skills of a number of fine employees over the years. These are highlighted throughout this history. More recently a well-developed human resources effort within DBC has been born, highlighted by the publication of a *DBC Employees' Handbook* (first edition) in 2010. Trustee David Hawkins played a major collaborative role in facilitating the writing of this manual.

14. I began DOCTOR OF MINISTRY studies through Dallas
    Seminary in the fall of 2003. I had contemplated beginning
    DMin studies for some time and had completed an application
    twice to enter the DMin program at Gordon-Conwell
    Theological Seminary in South Hamilton, Massachusetts.
    It was however, during one of three Bible conferences in
    DBC in which we hosted Dr. Ron Blue of Dallas Seminary
    as the main speaker that he suggested I apply to DTS's
    program. It was one of those moments of clarity in thinking
    that God's will became a clear path for me to pursue more
    graduate studies. I have always participated in continuing
    education and many seminars, and the church agreed to
    fund the DMin studies on a semester-by-semester basis,
    evaluating the usefulness of the program regularly. DBC
    was willing to finance the acquisition of this degree over five
    years. The doctor of ministry degree is designed to benefit
    the minister's own church as well as provide challenge and
    enrichment to the minister. Sensing a good opportunity
    through the DMin program to polish my preaching
    methodology, I enrolled and completed three preaching
    courses as part of the DMin program, two with renowned
    professor of preaching Dr. Haddon Robinson. I graduated
    from the doctor of ministry program at Dallas Theological
    Seminary in May 2008, accompanied by Renée, Jocelyn,
    and Susanna. It was a highlight and great blessing to have
    my family with me.

    I was "hooded" in Dallas by my program advisor, Dr. John
    Reed (also director of the doctor of ministry program) and
    encouraged by Drs. Howard Hendricks and Chuck Swindoll
    (who calls me "Massachusetts" when he sees me!). I loved the
    program and am grateful to DBC for making it possible. I
    hope it has benefited the church in some small ways.

Receiving the Doctor of Ministry hood from Dr. John Reed

15. IN 2008 DBC CELEBRATED OUR TWENTY-FIFTH ANNIVERSARY IN THE CHURCH with an evening attended by many friends and colleagues in ministry. It was much appreciated by both Renée and me. In attendance were Rev. Ken and Adele Nanfelt, Dr. Eric and Susan Sweitzer (Charis Counseling Center), Rev. Bob and Judy Pardon (New England Institute for Religious Research), Dominick and Dawn DeLuca (long-time friends of DBC), and Rev. Paul Hubley (District Executive Minister for the Northeast District of the Baptist General Conference.)

Left to Right: Susan Sweitzer, Judy Pardon, Rev. Bob Pardon,
Neil, Dr. Eric Sweitzer, Renée, Rev. Ken Nanfelt, Rev. Paul
Hubley, Dawn & Dominick DeLuca, Bill Hallett Jr.

16. Appointment to Protestant Chaplain for the University
of Massachusetts at Dartmouth, came to me in June 2007
by Dr. Susan Costa, Vice Chancellor for Student Affairs. I
have greatly enjoyed volunteering as part of the university's
"Religious Resource Center." I had supported campus
Christian community ministries ever since my arrival at
DBC in 1983, but I was especially delighted to be offered
a more formal staff position, if only as a very part-time
volunteer. In a sense, I followed in the footsteps of Don
Anderson, who also served there in this capacity for a short
while. Little noticed within DBC itself, this appointment
has been one of my greatest joys, and I am grateful for the
church allowing me to serve there. It has been my hope that
the church would feel some joy and pride in this "open door"
for the ministry of the gospel. In DBC's fiftieth year, UMD

will receive its first full-time workers with CRU (Campus Crusade for Christ) in 2011, UMD graduates Matthew and Rebecca Litchfield. That Renée and I could have some small part in helping this to happen has been a great joy and privilege. It is a highlight for our time in Dartmouth. Before too long, we also hope to see Intervarsity Christian Fellowship establish a staff worker in the UMD community for the first time. This is being advanced currently. I have established a good working relationship with Greg Johnson, the southeastern Massachusetts director for IVCF.

My wife's Renée's partnership with me through the years has been my greatest asset. It has not been appreciated how important her ministry behind the scenes has been over almost three decades here by my side. Renée has shared in the ministry of DBC in Vacation Bible School, teaching Sunday School, leading the Awana Sparks program for 10 years, hosting and co-leading couples' study and fellowship groups in our home, joining me in giving pre-marital counseling and assistance to couples, visitation alongside me with church families countless times, hosting overnight church guests in our home and enduring hard issues and episodes in the church's history. In numerous ways, Renée has quietly served and modeled just being a faithful church member with all the general ministries in DBC and throughout the chapters of church growth we have seen. She played an important role behind the scenes in prayerful support of all the church's major events and changes, in faithful love of her husband and children, and in carefully nurturing them in the things of the Lord. As do many pastors' wives, Renée endured many things over the years as well, especially early in our ministry, yet she has remained cheerful and ready to help in every way available to her. She would say her greatest ministry in DBC has been taking care of its pastor! This could not be more true.

Every pastor manages and absorbs criticisms over the time of his ministry. For that reason alone (and there are others), I was often told before arrival in Dartmouth, "If you can do anything else, do it!" Over time, the job description changes (whether you are aware of it or not); the needs of church members shift, the culture experiences changes, and your own capacity for challenge might weaken with age. If anything, I have become all too aware of my own shortcomings and inadequacies as a pastor. This is in part because there is always someone around to inform you of them, in part because your basic insecurities and fears whisper "defeat" to you, and in part because there *are* some actually in place! Because of my awareness of these disappointments, I have sought to stay close to a number of other pastors and leaders. It is a "driver" of why I have always enjoyed returning to Dallas Seminary for short courses and seminars over the years and in many other places as well.

I have needed encouragement, refreshment, and continuing education on a regular basis. I cannot imagine doing without these assets. But if I have learned a single lesson, it is the need to fall back on the basic conviction that God has called me to do this work. My task was to get the training, to keep a teachable heart, and to just obey God's leadings. God's task is to sustain me and my wife through the challenges and criticisms and to keep them in perspective. That it is the simple nature of shepherding. The sheep will bite sometimes, and God has yet to call into ministry a perfect person. So I have kept my focus on grace in my theology and in my ministry. It is by His good calling and grace that I could do anything for Christ's kingdom.

I have often reflected in recent years that I am as surprised as anyone that the Lord has kept us in Dartmouth for so many years. I also am not always sure why He has done so—but one thing is plain: He clearly has. During 1994 to 1996, I sought placement in other parts of the country. Renée and I prayed much in that time and interviewed in several other states. However, the Lord plainly had another plan. He desired us to stay in Dartmouth. When we surrendered to that plan, there was a sense of God's blessing on us and our children that has sustained us through many later challenges. Between that time and the present, our church has doubled in size. We have constructed a new facility, added many missionaries, explored new opportunities to become more visible in the community and develop connections, grown our staff, and advanced the gospel. The Lord receives all the credit, but we have received joy to see Him work. Our willingness to remain in Dartmouth continues as long as He blesses our ministries.

Chapter 7

KEY COUPLES, INDIVIDUALS, AND MINISTRIES

For as the body is one, and hath many members, and
all the members of that one body, being many, are one
body: so also is Christ. (1ˢᵗ Corinthians 12:12)

It almost seems futile to try to mention with any fairness all the
people who have made a significant contribution to DBC over
its five decades. Undoubtedly some will be inadvertently forgotten,
though the contributions and faithfulness of all are appreciated. A
few DBC members, however, deserve some mention because they
made DBC their church home for at least twenty years, used their
spiritual gifts faithfully, endured challenging times with patience,
and treated their fellow church members as true family members.
These include the following.

RUTH DURFEE NOLAN

Ruth Durfee Nolan is a very special member of our church and continues to be important to us as we approach the fiftieth anniversary of DBC's founding in her living room. After the death of her husband, Rev. Chaloner Durfee, Ruth later married Mr. Richard Nolan, and their wedding ceremony was celebrated by Rev. Mel Longtin, DBC's fourth pastor. Unfortunately Richard Nolan passed away, and although Ruth endured the loss of two husbands, she continued in warm faithfulness to her sons and their families and to DBC. In 1992 she and Associate Pastor Parascand began the SWAT ministry (Senior Women Alone Together), which she continued leading until her declining health required her to step back in 2011. SWAT (a term originated collaboratively by Ruth and Rev. Lou Parascand) is one of DBC's longest-running ministries. Also Ruth's son Bruce and his family worshipped and served in DBC for many years.

WILLIAM SR. AND DOROTHY HALLETT

Bill Sr. and his wife, Dorothy, were both raised in Dartmouth and in 1963 were members of the First Christian Church of Hixville. With the planting of the Dartmouth Baptist Fellowship, the Halletts became charter members, along with their sons, Bill Jr. and James. Bill played the organ, and Dorothy kept the books. Their faithfulness and dedication to the work saw DBC through lean and sometimes stressful times. They are remembered for their hard work and determination and love for the gospel through the early years of the new church. Their final visit to DBC came during the dedication of the new facility in 2000. Bill Sr. went home to be with the Lord in August 2003 and Dorothy in January 2006.

MR. GUY LUMPKIN, PASTORAL INTERN (1987)

During 1987, DBC began to slowly take a turn for growth and transitioning from difficult times. I received a telephone call in the spring of 1987 from third-year Dallas Seminary student Guy Lumpkin (originally from San Diego) inquiring about the possibility of doing a pastoral internship at DBC. Guy was planning to be working as a bridge carpenter that summer on the Braga Bridge in Fall River and wondered if he could also work part-time as a pastoral intern at DBC. He and wife Terry and son Daniel came to Dartmouth, and Guy completed the internship and decided to stay an additional three months in DBC. During his six months at Dartmouth Bible Church, Guy taught a mid-week "Introduction to New Testament Greek" class (his concentration at DTS), preached, and shepherded people. He and his family became permanent residents of Dallas upon his graduation from the seminary and remain good friends of mine today. The Lumpkins have graciously hosted me many times when I was working on the DMin and after for short courses at the seminary.

RON AND CHERYL GALLEGOS (1988–1994, 2002 ON ...)

In the summer of 1988, a new young couple, Ron and Cheryl Gallegos, relocated to New Bedford from Nebraska. They began attending and subsequently joined Dartmouth Bible Church. Ron and Cheryl added much-needed musical ability and skills in children's ministry. They generously provided time and love to our church until Ron was transferred (by the FAA) to Republic, Missouri, in the summer of 1994. Subsequently, the Gallegos's entered full-time Christian work with Victory Ministries at Camp Li-Wa ("Living Water") in Fairbanks, Alaska. In 2004, DBC added them to our growing missionary budget and to the list of missionaries for whom we regularly pray. The Gallegos's have been back to visit Dartmouth several times, and our affection for them remains great. Rachel Donner, a young adult member of our own church, volunteered at Camp Li-Wa during the summer of 2007, and in 2011, Renée and I visited Ron and Cheryl at Camp Li-Wa. In 2012, DBC sent a work team of seven adults to provide work support at Camp Li-Wa.

STEUART AND CAROL BAILEY

We first met Steuart and Carol Bailey when they were still members of Elim Baptist Church and before our merger with that church. Since 1991, Steuart has served DBC as a deacon, as our most tenured elder, as a Sunday School teacher, and as a small group leader, and he has been generally available to help any and all who request it. He has performed hundreds of visits and is a man of prayer, and joins that with a keen wit and sense of humor. Carol is multi-gifted and has marked DBC with many ministries to children and hospitality, and all with much creativity. She was on our first worship team and has graciously served as a willing host to many out-of-town guests of DBC. The Baileys are missions enthusiasts and have been invaluable on our Windows to the World team. Carol has a special ability in the area of one-time projects, which she engages with great enthusiasm and commitment. This is a love and aptitude for single and short-duration ministry projects, undertaken with great verve and focus to completion. In addition, Steuart's and Carol's daughters, Nicole and

Rebekah, who have grown up in our church, have vigorously served Dartmouth Bible Church in many ways and are greatly loved and appreciated by everyone in the body. One can hardly imagine more valuable and delightful church members.

MICHAEL AND LYNN BROWN

We first met Mike and Lynn and their children, Chad and Lisa, when they attended The First Christian Church of Hixville. The Browns had come to faith in Christ in 1981 and began attending Dartmouth Bible Church in 1991. They quickly became regular attenders and valued members in our fellowship. Michael joined DBC in 1993, followed by Lynn some years later. In 2001, Lynn was hired as part-time church secretary. Mike has served as a trustee and is a great prayer supporter. He has rendered countless hours of help to DBC in the area of heating, ventilation, and air conditioning. His passion is in the area of eschatology (end times theology), and he was instrumental in our bringing Dr. Jimmy DeYoung to DBC as a conference speaker in 2011. Both Mike and Lynn are much loved in DBC, and Lynn has had a ministry with many people in and around DBC as church secretary, helper, and friend.

JONATHAN AND DEBBIE DONNER

Jon Donner and his wife, Debbie, have been an important part of the DBC family for almost twenty years. Debbie grew up in Calvary Bible Church, and Jon grew up in Middleboro, the son of missionary parents, Rev. Oliver "Hap" and Betty Donner, who were long-time and beloved members of Central Baptist Church. Jon spent his senior year of high school on the mission field in Kenya and then attended Liberty University. Debbie, a registered nurse, attended the Philadelphia College of the Bible and then nursing school. Jon's gift in the area of worship leading and song writing has been appreciated in DBC for many years. Jon has served in many helping ministries and in the Men's Ministry of DBC as well. Debbie began two current DBC ministries: the "Prayer Room" ministry and our Health Team, for which she took "parish nurse" training over eight months in Fall River.

Two of Jon and Debbie's children, Rachel and Aaron, have contributed significantly to DBC's ministry too. The Donners' older daughter, Sarah, relocated to New Jersey, but both Rachel and Aaron have remained in our area. Each of them has participated in several short-term missions trips, worked with children and teens in DBC, and served in the Upper Room (now "Strive") Twenties ministry. Aaron has also shared his gifts in the area of music. The Donners have always been a bright spot in the life of Dartmouth Bible Church.

Brendan and Barbara Gahan

Brendan and Barbara Gahan began attending DBC from Swansea in 1990—just before we began exploring the merger with Elim Baptist Church. I had originally met Brendan when I spoke in chapel at Christian Day in Fall River in 1985, where Brendan was a teacher. Brendan owned and managed a Christian book store called "The Living Room," which was located in Swansea, Massachusetts. He visited our church with his book-table ministry, and then he and Barbara began attending Dartmouth Bible Church together and quickly became valued and much-loved members. Brendan has served as an elder, leader of the LCs ministry to older men, adult Sunday School teacher, small group leader, greeter, and friend to many. His obvious gift of encouragement, paired with Barbara's keen administrative abilities, give DBC two much-appreciated leaders. Barbara served as Christian Education Coordinator, co-chair of the

Women's Ministry Team in recent years, and as Chairperson of the Building Committee for our new facility (the only woman I have known to serve in such a capacity!) She has served in many other ways as well, faithfully and cheerfully without fail. It is providential that at a time when DBC was growing, the Lord would provide these new leaders at just the right time.

WILLIAM JR. AND HOPE HALLETT

Bill Hallett Jr. is a charter member of DBC and was active in church ministry in the 1960s and '70s. One of five Vietnam War veterans currently in DBC, Bill stands as a respected and appreciated servant of both his country and the kingdom of God. In more recent years, Bill has served as a deacon, elder, usher, Sunday School teacher, and preacher. Bill has brought to DBC a combination much needed by any church today: that singular sense of balance in all things wed to a lighthearted sense of humor. Hope Hallett, Bill's wife, has served on our worship team and has brought us many insights from her activism as a Christian in the public arena. Hope has also a great example to us of someone using her nursing skills and long experience with a mindset for the kingdom.

DAVID AND VIVIAN HAWKINS

David and Vivian (Mingola) Hawkins have ministered in numerous ways. David began attending Dartmouth Bible Church while he was a student at SMU. He met Vivian, who grew up in New Bedford and began attending DBC in the early 1980s. David has served as the financial team chairman, as a trustee, and as the chairman of the trustees. He served as Awana commander since 1989, the second year of that ministry in DBC. He has been instrumental in helping DBC become compliant with state and federal regulations for nonprofit organizations. David has developed our financial accountability and systemization, enhanced our technological capabilities in many ways, and spearheaded the development of employee protocols. Vivian has served faithfully throughout Awana's long twenty-five-year history in DBC and in many other capacities as well. The Hawkins family—including David's mother, Emily (who relocated from Springfield to Dartmouth in 2002), and their three sons (Billy, Stephen, and Drew)—have been a faithful, hardworking, and exemplary part of the body at DBC for over twenty-five years. Billy Hawkins created and has maintained our church website for several years. As a result of his hard work, DBC receives more visitors from this asset than from any other form of advertising.

Reverend David and Ruth Schaffer

Reverend David Schaffer and his wife Ruth came to Elim Baptist Church from Connecticut in 1972. David was a Boston University graduate, BU Divinity School graduate, and later a graduate also of Bethel Theological Seminary. Ruth was trained and worked as a registered nurse. Their two children, Elizabeth and Mark, grew up in Elim Baptist Church. Even with their transition out of the Elim pastorate and into nursing home chaplaincy (Community Chaplain Service, founded by another former Elim pastor, David Kimball), David and Ruth kept their membership in Elim and became Dartmouth Bible Church members at the time of the merger. They have served as notable prayer enthusiasts and since 1995 have maintained a significant ministry among foreign students and faculty at UMass Dartmouth. They have offered an English-as-a-Second-Language (ESL) class since 1995 and have worked with people from China, Taiwan, Japan, Vietnam, and other countries. They have been much loved by the international community as well as by all in DBC and have served as consistent mentors and reflections of the Lord Jesus. In addition, the Schaffers have served on DBC's missions group, Windows to the World, as part of the worship team, and have happily enjoyed their son Mark's support, who has also been an occasional attender at DBC. Renée and I also fondly remember the Schaffers' befriending us early, when we first came to DBC. David read many stories to our girls when they were young! Too much honor and appreciation cannot be given to this fine gift of a couple to Dartmouth Bible Church and to our entire region.

TOM AND KATHIE MARGINSON

Tom and Kathie Marginson have served the Lord and DBC for many years. The Marginsons were married in 1980 by DBC's third pastor, Ray Leavitt, at Elim Baptist Church. Kathie, however, had been in DBC since 1971. Except for a two-year period during which Kathie worked for the Baptist General Conference headquarters in Chicago, she has served wonderfully in DBC in many ways for almost four decades. Tom was a career firefighter in New Bedford, retiring with distinction at the rank of District Chief in 2008. Kathie has served as a trustee, women's ministry teacher, in Awana Clubs and as a Sunday School teacher. Tom has given use of his gifts in video production, served in the sound room, helping many times with grounds work, ushering and in teaching in our Awana Clubs and Sunday School as well. His humble and steady presence and friendship of many have served us all well. Kathie also served faithfully over several years on our New Building Committee and occasionally providing legal direction when we have needed it. She and Tom have simply desired to be faithful servants of the Lord Jesus Christ. Also, Tom and Kathie's son, Jonathan, created our church's second website after his graduation from UMass Dartmouth, which we used for two years. It was my privilege to perform the wedding ceremony for him and wife, Danielle, in September 2011. On a lighter note, Jonathan is the originator and "commissioner" of DBC's Fantasy Football League.

BOB AND JOAN WHITLOW

Robert Whitlow and his wife, Joan, came into DBC in 1978. Unswerving in their faithfulness to DBC through the trying years of the early 1980s, Bob and Joan both ministered faithfully in numerous ways for many years. Bob served as a prototype elder briefly in the earliest days of our having elders and then fully as such from 1991 until 2009, and more recently as Men's Ministries leader. He also served at various times as a deacon, youth leader, small group leader, church electrician, Sunday School teacher, treasurer, musician, and worship leader. Joan has served wonderfully for many years on the Women's Ministry team, as a children's worker, and as a deaconess. The Whitlows have exemplified that popular measure of Christian discipleship: faithful, available, teachable. Their son Matthew and his wife, Megan, also served in many ways over the years as faithful members and helpers in many ministries. Megan began the MOPS (Mothers of Pre-Schoolers) ministry at DBC in 2008. The dedication and service of the Whitlow family is much appreciated and held in high regard by many people in and outside of the DBC community.

JOHN AND ELIZABETH ZARECKI

John and Elizabeth came to DBC regularly after the Franklin Graham Crusade in New Bedford in October 1993. The Zareckis quickly found ways to help and serve in DBC from their earliest months in our church. John has served as an intrepid elder, enthusiastic Hospitality team chairman, cheerful greeter, careful Sunday School teacher, devoted LCs shepherd and in many other ways as a true "churchman." Elizabeth has served as Sunday School Coordinator, Sunday School teacher, in nursery, as a deaconess and in hospitality in many ways, including the Welcome Luncheons. Elizabeth's indefatigable cheerfulness and joy in the Lord has blessed DBC immeasurably. The Zareckis' hunger for God's Word and eagerness to grow in grace have blessed DBC greatly. Their sons, Dominic and Alexander, are also very special and valuable to DBC and special to me as fellow New Bedford High School Band "Whalers" to our daughters! It was my privilege to perform the wedding ceremony for Dominic and wife, Esther, in July 2011 in Pasadena, California. In 2012 Alexander has again found himself in DBC, and we look forward to his unfolding ministries for Christ among us!

RECENT YEARS:
OTHER COUPLES AND INDIVIDUALS

There have been a large number of additional people who have made a deep impact on DBC, many of whom have served in our church for more than twenty years. *Bob Graham* and his late wife, *Nancy Graham,* ministered long and hard in DBC. When we arrived in Dartmouth, the Grahams were far and away the oldest couple in the church, and they were only in their mids! Bob served for many years as both a deacon and as a trustee. He assisted on many projects (including invaluable service on the New Building Committee throughout our long facility expansion). Nancy served as Church Clerk for many years, until she went home to be with the Lord in 2002. Bob and Nancy hosted a small group Thursday night Bible study in their home, which I led for six years. Over one hundred people came to the Grahams' home at one time or another to study God's Word together in those years.

Shirley Barboza first attended DBC in 1970 with her husband,

Frank, neither being regular churchgoers previously. Shirley related in 2012 that they found the Lord through the ministry of DBC. Shirley stayed until 1976 and then returned in 1989 and has ministered faithfully from then until now. She has served as church clerk, in our Awana ministry, as a deaconess, and in many other ways, with much appreciation from the body.

Ron and Susan (Blenkhorn) Brunette have served in many ministries including deacon, deaconess, Sunday School, chair set-up, coffee house, and hosting many youth events at their home. Susan was an SMU student (class of 1984) and one of the first to attend DBC during my ministry. The Brunettes' cheerfulness and faithfulness are some of our greatest assets. Also possessed of a remarkable gift of diplomacy, Ron has been helpful in stressful moments, which every church endures from time to time. Susan's mother, *Ruth Blenkhorn,* came to DBC from Milton, Massachusetts, and is much loved among us. She possesses a great love for Bible study and working in Awana and a keen dedication to missions through serving on our Windows to the World team.

John and Betty Aanensen came to DBC in October 1986, having moved from California. Each served in DBC in numerous ways and with distinction. Their children, Erik, Marlies, Sonja, and Karen, each left a happy mark in our church and indeed are all still seen in DBC from time to time.

Donald and Lubelia Clapp have been a blessing in DBC for many years—Donald as an elder and Sunday School teacher and very approachable friend to many and Lubelia on our Women's Ministry team. Donald (a Vietnam War veteran) used his photographic skills to help create a photo directory. Both have been part of our foundational strength for a long time!

Barry Mingola has served as a deacon and in the men's ministry and is always appreciated for his sense of humor and good insights. As a combat Vietnam veteran, the lessons he learned there later fortified his determination to follow the Lord Jesus.

Judy Lemieux came to DBC with Elim and has served as Treasurer, Trustee and has been providing janitorial service for a number of years. As the lone Christian in her family for many years, she has powerfully exemplified courage and determination to follow the Lord Jesus.

Few have so consistently brought cheerfulness and encouragement to DBC as has *Bonnie Furtado*. In addition, she bore up in the Lord's strength in the loss of her son, still served in our Awana program many years, and brought her wonderful sister into DBC, Maureen Blackledge (from New Hampshire). She also ministers especially among our senior women, organizing an annual luncheon for them for several years. Bonnie is one of our real gems, and we thank the Lord for her.

Noelia Murphy came into DBC in the early 1990s, accompanied by husband, Michael, sons, Michael and Christopher, and daughter, Amanda. Noelia has served effectively as our junior high Sunday School teacher for fifteen years, and we have appreciated her ministry there immensely.

Bob Reed is the sole DBC member of the Reed family that was part of the church in the earliest days. Growing up in Calvary Bible Church, Bob has faithfully ministered in DBC's Awana Clubs, in small groups, in Sunday School, and in other ways for many years. His late wife, Cathy, was also appreciated and loved in our church.

Dr. Dean Schmidlin served in many ways for over twenty-four years, including as a focused and gifted elder, Sunday School teacher, counter, and good friend to many. He is mentioned elsewhere in this history.

Breslin and Janet Marlowe first attended DBC in 1968 and moved to Calvary Bible Church and then back to DBC in the early 1990s. The Marlowes have been much-appreciated and faithful members since then. Their oldest son, Christopher, also attends as of this writing. Breslin went home to His Master on December 17th,

2012 but leaves behind a rich legacy of love for local history. I regret this book was not completed in time for him to read it.

Maureen Morency Saunders first attended DBC in 1985 while part of a Barrington College chorale. She and her husband, *Tom,* have been part of DBC for many years now, with Maureen serving in our Women's Ministry, Worship Team and as a deaconess. Tom served on Worship Team and as a deacon, and both have helped DBC in many ways. Maureen's late mother, *Peggy Morency* and sister, *Diane,* also became part of DBC at her invitation. Maureen and Tom raised two sons, Bob and Dan, in DBC, who are both loved and appreciated.

Cathy Shorrock and her father, *Ray St. Don,* came to us from Elim in the 1991 merger and are much-beloved servants in our church! Cathy is co-chair of our Women's Ministry Team for many years now and has hosted a Bible study in her home for years, and Ray has served as an usher and as a counter. Ray's cheerful steadiness was helpful in the early days of our merger with Elim. Both father and daughter have always exemplified the servant's heart, and while each has endured the death of spouses, each has remained tender-hearted to the Lord.

Donna Wingrove has blessed us with a love for Awana as a Cubbies leader for many years, as a Sunday School teacher, and on our first worship team for a number of years, too. Donna worked hard to earn Awana's Meritorious Award in 1998, a great example as a leader!

Frank and Madeline Sinclair came to DBC in the fall of 1983, the first visitors under my ministry to stay long term in our church. Frank and Madeline hosted many ministries in their home in Westport in the late 1980s and all through the 1990s, and Frank was one of our first permanent elders. He served until he went home to be with the Lord in 2001. Madeline has a great heart for evangelism and touched many lives with the gospel. Frank and Madeline also facilitated our bowling league with much enthusiasm during its run for several years in the 1990s. At least two people found the bowling league to be a "normal" point of entry into the life of our church.

Although not with us twenty years yet, *Dr. Larry and Fran Logan* deserve some mention, as do *Robert and Valorie Schofield*. Both of these senior couples came to DBC from Calvary Bible Church in that church's difficult time in 2002. Larry has served invaluably in DBC as an elder, Sunday School teacher, greeter, and encourager in many ways. Fran has served as a greeter and has a special burden to assist at baptisms! Her service is much loved and has demonstrated to us a new way of loving the body. Larry and Fran have also shown us two people with a great love of learning and for studying God's Word. Probably no one has taken more classes, read more books, or asked more probing questions than has this couple. They also served as fine examples of family-faithfulness as they cared in their home for Larry's parents, Rev. Villa and Maudie Hall, until each went home to the Lord.

Bob Schofield came to us from Calvary Bible Church in 2002 after many decades of service there. Bob is a US Navy veteran of World War II from the crew of the light cruiser CL-103, USS Wilkes-Barre, with many inspiring stories. He has a real heart for both prayer and missions and has blessed DBC with a maturity that has quietly strengthened many. Bob's wife, *Valorie,* also has served DBC well since 2002 through Sunday School, missions involvement, and mentoring younger women. While I regretted Calvary's loss of the Schofields, I rejoiced in Dartmouth's gain.

Also coming to us from Calvary Bible Church for just three years were *Dr. Beryl Barkman* and *Mrs. Mary Barkman, esq.* Dr. Barkman was one of our first DIBS instructors and passed into the presence of the Lord in August of 2012 at ninety-five years of age. They relocated to Burlington, North Carolina, in 2003. His long career, first as a naval gunnery officer on a submarine during World War II and then as a college professor for many years, was a great inspiration to many in DBC. Beryl and Mary related to me that their wedding was officiated by the famous A. W. Tozer during World War II, and Dr. Barkman was also a great mentor to Dr. Larry Logan.

Rev. Bill and Carol Stack have been a great blessing in DBC for ten years. Bill, a former U.S. Air Force electronics airman and originally from Charlestown, Massachusetts, is a graduate of the Citadel Bible College and the Southern Baptist Theological Seminary, Boston extension. He is the former pastor, on *two* occasions, of the Haven Baptist Church in New Bedford and has served well as an elder in DBC, Sunday School teacher, small group leader, and also formerly a deacon and pulpit supply at Calvary Bible Church of Westport. Carol has a great gift of mercy and encouragement and has served in DBC as a very capable deaconess.

I need also to mention *Bob and Susan Bouley*, who also are under twenty years among us but still very valuable to the church in the 2000s. Bob has served as a Trustee, sound-room worker and with a shepherding heart, as an encourager both to new people and to older members. He also has a heart for prison ministry. Susan has served wonderfully on our worship team as a singer, violinist, and occasionally as substitute leader. Both Bob and Susan have made a significant impact in the lives of DBC people.

Sallie Wilson is also a relative newcomer to DBC but has been a great blessing to the church and served as Sunday School teacher, Women's Ministry Team member/hostess and Windows to the World member. Her maturity and experience in ministry have been immeasurable in their value to us! *Dr. Xiaoquin Shelley Zhang* and her husband *Liang Li* have been a blessing in DBC as our first mainland-born Chinese members! Shelley's quiet wisdom and Liang's service as a deacon, along with their two wonderful daughters, Danya and Joy, have added a special blessing to the life of DBC. With Shelley and Liang have come *Dr. Maolin Guo* and *Weiping Yang*. Each has blessed DBC in their own giftedness, and their children are growing up in our fellowship. As previously mentioned, *Dr. June Jiao* and her family came into DBC from graduate study in Kansas. Husband, *Dr. Wengung Che* who lives and works in China mostly, is in our church regularly when he is here visiting. Son Ben, now a student at Harvard University, has been a blessing to us as is younger son Robert.

Dr. Shuowei Cai has been nothing but a blessing. Coming to this country from the 13 million–person Chinese city of Tianjin, Shuowei came to Christ through the evangelistic ministry of Pastor Larry Swartz (Dartmouth Baptist Church). He has grown greatly in his faith and is a hungry student of God's Word. He is loved by all who know him and demonstrates a faithfulness to Christ that honors and blesses us all.

Finally, *Emma Griffin* ministered in DBC as our main pianist for many years. She came to us in the merger with Elim Baptist Church and cheerfully embraced a new, merged congregation. She grew up in Dedham, Massachusetts, and remembered life as far back as the town celebration for the ending of the First World War! Emma's faith and faithfulness—both to the Lord and to her husband, *Philip*—were a great addition to our church, and we miss her still, as she went into glory on June 12, 2005.

Colorful People

If I said, "There have been some colorful and interesting people in DBC over the years," someone would no doubt say, "Isn't everyone interesting?" I would reply, "Of course." Having touched base with that fact, now, I can say, "There have been some colorful and interesting people in DBC over the years." Some exceeded the normal threshold of interesting and brought a unique story to our midst, if only for a season, and made a marked impact on our church family. Some of these people are described below.

Emmanuel Pacheco, known as Manny, first visited DBC with friends Joe Tavares and Esther DaSilva in the fall of 1984. Manny had been a POW in the Second World War, having been captured during the Battle of the Bulge and marched into Germany, where he was interred at the Bad Orb prison camp until liberation in April 1945. Though he spent only four months as a POW, the experience was so terrible that it affected him for the rest of his life, and he was declared a 100 percent disabled veteran. We got to know Manny late in life, along with his wife, Julie, and son, Lenny. Manny loved the Lord and crafted a number of carpentry projects for DBC in the last years of his life. He and Julie also hosted the annual DBC summer picnic at their home for several years. Manny has been with the Lord since 2004, and we remember him as a generous man, anxious to serve and invested with a deep faith in the Lord Jesus Christ. *Joe Tavares* attended DBC and served joyfully for many years. *Esther DaSilva* also attended DBC regularly for a number of years.

George Frangu—In 1986 I received a telephone inquiry from World Relief, at that time the refugee ministry of the National Association of Evangelicals. They inquired if our church would be willing to sponsor a Romanian refugee to the United States. Without such a sponsorship, the refugee would not be granted admittance into the country. George F. came to DBC in the early fall, having swum across the Danube River to escape his country, which at that time was still oppressively Communist. Many people in DBC gave friendship and aid to George, who did not yet speak English. We also introduced him to the gospel. Bob and Nancy Graham, and Joe Tavares helped George in many ways, as did others in our church, and our ministry to George represented a new kind of personal outreach on both a spiritual and social level. Though he has been out of touch for many years now, we understand George lives in northern New England and married to his lifelong Romanian sweetheart.

Christine Ferguson—Chris came into DBC and ministered with great love and affection for a number of years until relocating to Connecticut in 1997. Chris has a profound gift of hospitality and visitation and made a place for herself in the lives of many in DBC.

It was Chris who first showed friendliness to *Caroline Louis*, who visited DBC several times before anyone noticed her! Caroline grew up in Malaysia (with her twin sister *Henrietta*) and has been for many years now a British subject and citizen of London. She spent a year in Dartmouth as an exchange occupational therapist at St. Luke's Hospital and attended DBC. She and Henrietta (also an occupational therapist in London) are members of the famous All Souls Church there and have a great heart for missions. They have served on numerous short-term missions trips in various difficult and needy parts of the world and showed me great hospitality when I visited London in 2001.

It was Caroline's friend, *Stuart Tanner*, research associate to the famous First Minister of Northern Ireland, Ian Paisley, in Belfast, who housed me and extended great kindness to me when I visited that city. MP Paisley commissioned his personal secretary to grant me (with Stuart) a personal tour of Parliament on that visit, including a look at Parliament's own copy of *Magna Carta*! Stuart visited DBC for a weekend and played piano for us, as a gifted concert pianist.

Willio Destin, from Haiti, was an undergraduate student at UMass Dartmouth and also the president of the Christian Fellowship there and a part of DBC for his four years here. He subsequently attended and graduated from The Master's Seminary in Sun Valley, California, and hopes to return with wife *Neecole* to Haiti to minister there. Willio led the one short-term missions trip I have been on (so far) to Grand Goave, Haiti, in 2006 which DBC supported.

Lisa Robinson is the other person who went to seminary from DBC, and she is currently enrolled in Dallas Seminary's Master of

Theology program. When Lisa became a part of DBC in 2007, she presented an exceptional mind and capacity for theological study, and I encouraged her to consider graduate studies at DTS, to which I added my recommendation for her application.

Edwin Menon, 2004 UMD graduate and another former UMD Christian Fellowship president, has become a good friend of DBC in recent years. At this writing he is a rising first-year Master of Divinity student at Gordon-Conwell Theological Seminary and a regular speaker in the DBC pulpit. From Singapore originally, Edwin has blessed DBC, and we look for great things from his ministry in years to come.

Finally, I mention the presence at one time or another of various people with all kinds of complex problems who have touched our hearts. *Prison inmates, transsexuals,* and *street people* from Dartmouth have been in DBC for a short or longer periods of time. Nothing is harder than watching one of the people in our church become convicted of a crime and go to jail. This is especially true if that person is a professing Christian. But in the three cases that we have seen, each person maintained his Christian faith through the trials and incarcerations, and that itself is a testimony to the reality of the Christian faith. In the case of people from other sexual "lifestyles" (than heterosexual), we have worked to receive them graciously and patiently, always seeking to address the spiritual issues. We have been challenged by the gravity of the issues at stake but always sought to answer the concerns as we imagine the Lord Jesus would have done. Also, over the years homeless people of various levels of need have come to DBC for help. We have sought in those cases to meet every need we could, all the while seeking to help them spiritually as well.

No one could accuse DBC of ignoring people from the harder parts of society, and periodically our church has reached out and ministered to severely troubled individuals. We hope that by God's grace we have presented and demonstrated the Lord Jesus in at least an approximately accurate fashion.

Chapter 8

WHERE ARE WE
GOING FROM HERE?

Brethren, I count not myself to have apprehended: but
this one thing I do, forgetting those things which are
behind, and reaching forth unto those things which are
before, I press toward the mark for the prize of the high
calling of God in Christ Jesus. (Philippians 3:13,14)

Where does a church go from where it is? On the one hand,
it might seem presumptuous for Christians—as fragile as
we tend to be—to believe that we can reliably speculate or project
any pattern as to how God is leading us. On the other hand, is it
not a lack of faith and joy (and even a little cynical) to simply sit
and wait to see whatever happens? "Where are we going next?" and
"How is God leading us?" are fundamental questions that all church
leaders (or simply *Christians*) need to prayerfully explore. God leads
churches in some years to press on, make bold plans, and seek
resources to carry out those plans—and then in other years, to wait,
build stability, and simply "disciple" the members we have.

DBC has generally been driven to seek the mind of Christ
and follow His leading on growth. In 1963 Pastor Durfee boldly

envisioned a church in the proximity of a college, the ground for which had not even yet been broken. Fifteen years later, the leaders switched from the traditional polity and worship to a more progressive methodology. This took some courage. Another dozen years went by, and two groups of believers (DBC and Elim) joined their smaller churches together in hopes of building a better base from which to grow and make an impact for the gospel. This called for a fresh vision. Then there were seven more years before DBC was able to proceed with tripling facility space, which required trust in God, a faith-born confidence in His provision, and a willingness to "risk." Another decade came and saw the multiplication of staff in DBC, demanding more vision. In between all these relatively few "bold moves" to grow, lay long years of "ministry as usual," watching God lead in each step. In those times our congregation hopefully learned how the Lord guides and that whether moving or waiting, certain priorities are perpetually relevant:

- He *always* wants us to seek and promote His glory and to live in ways that invite His manifold presence in our midst.
- He *always* wants us to evangelize (because the New Testament makes this so clear—four apostles inform us in Matt. 28:19–20; Acts 1:8; 1 Cor. 9:19–23; 1 Peter 3:15). We are to do so with all the creativity and energy and innovation we can find.
- He *always* wants us to explore how to love one another, build each other up, and forgive and protect and nurture each other. The mandate to encourage each other does not expire.
- He *always* wants us to praise Him and to pray. Paul tells us to do this "without ceasing."
- He *always* wants us to teach His Word faithfully, to disciple our own children and families, and to deepen our love for the truth and an orthodox theology.

These five general priorities are timeless and know no boundaries of nation or race. They are more than priorities—they are *urgencies*. But as noted in the beginning of this book, even though they begin with the best of intentions, most churches do not last beyond a few decades. More churches live for a time and then come to an end than those that thrive and continually grow. We see that a church organization is not an end unto itself. Even though its members love their beautiful buildings and their rich heritages, Jesus' words to Nicodemus are ever true: "The wind blows where it wishes and we hear the sound of it, but do not know where it comes from and where it is going; so is everyone who is born of the Spirit" (John 3:8). We must acknowledge a certain sovereignty to how the Spirit really moves and we do not desire to be presumptuous and to "think more highly of ourselves than we ought to" (Rom.12:3). We cannot presume that we deserve to be used of Him indefinitely. Conversely, there is really no limit to how the Spirit *might* use believers to magnify the reputation of the Lord Jesus Christ and to add to His body as He sees fit, if that body seeks righteousness and desires more than anything to listen to His voice! To intentionally limit the size of the Lord's community by having a smaller vision would be just as presumptuous as to be overconfident.

Several times over the years DBC has crafted "strategic plans," lists of goals, and visionary statements. When I arrived in 1983, I quickly learned that the recent switch-over from traditional Baptist ministry to a more progressive evangelicalism was fueled by a fresh striving to discover and do things biblically and *only* biblically. Renée and I came to DBC from Trinity Fellowship and Believer's Chapel in Dallas (much larger churches, both of a Plymouth Brethren flavor, defined by that same "biblical only" philosophy.) We were married, and I was trained and ordained in Grace Church in Roanoke, Virginia, known in the Roanoke Valley at in the mid-1970s as a very progressive and biblical congregation, set apart from the denominational stuffiness of that region.

In DBC this progressive talk perplexed the older people who founded the church, even though ironically they had founded the church with that same impetus (albeit in 1963!). They were told that *new* models provided by the Fellowship Bible Churches of Texas and the Grace Community Church (California) of Gene Getz and John MacArthur, respectively, offered clearer and more powerful examples of what DBC should emulate. That Getz was in Texas and MacArthur in California—states full of evangelical strength and large numbers of wealthy and strong Christians—mattered little to the young leaders of those days. DBC's growth happened—but only very slowly, with the fatigue and departure of most of those early 1980s leaders.

Currently our conference identifies with the following description:

> *Converge* is a fellowship of Baptist churches whose theology is biblically evangelical; whose character is multi-ethnic; whose spirit is positive and affirmative; whose purpose is to fulfill the Great Commission through evangelism, discipleship, and church planting; and whose people celebrate openness and freedom in the context of Christ's Lordship[25]

Converge's Purpose Statement reads:

> The purpose of *Converge* is to glorify God by encouraging its district Baptist General Conference churches to fulfill the Great Commandment (Mark 12:29-30) and the Great Commission (Matthew 28:19-20) of Jesus Christ.[26]

DBC's own Purpose Statement reads:

> The reason for the existence of Dartmouth Bible Church is

---

[25] Identity Statement, *Constitution and By-Laws for The Northeast Baptist Conference,* revision draft, Sept. 14, 2012, 2.

[26] Purpose Statement, *Ibid*, 3.

to honor God by growing in our relationship with Him and with one another, through a balanced focus on worship, discipleship, fellowship, ministry and evangelism.[27]

These three descriptions capture well the aspiration and hope of our church for ministry into the future.

Some of our individual leaders over the years were more strategic in their thinking; others were more traditionally minded. I lean toward the latter, although I have attended many seminars, read many books, and listened to many preachers touting the value and even the spirituality of thinking conceptually and entrepreneurially about church growth. Another factor was that none of the first seven pastors of DBC stayed longer than three and a half years. No one can "grow" a church to any extent with only a brief pastorate. And while some may feel that a more gifted first long-term pastor than I would have stimulated quicker growth (and I would be among those), it is true also that in this part of the country, much patience is needed. It has been my privilege to know several long-term pastors in this area: the late Rev. Dr. Manuel Chavier, Pastor Ken Nanfelt, Pastor Joseph Biddle, Dr. Ron Larson, and Pastor Paul Hubley. Each would say that a sustained pastoral ministry requires determination, commitment, and patience (and indeed, these qualities among the church people too). Few churches over the past 150 years in South Coast, Massachusetts, have grown dramatically in a short time.

A SAFE HAVEN

An almost indiscernible reality that unfolded in DBC was that we seemed, quite undeliberately, to have become a "safe haven" for Christians who had been wounded or injured in other religious settings, including other churches. We did not set out to become

---

[27] Dartmouth Bible Church, *Constitution and By-Laws,* February 8, 2004 Edition, 12.

such a "city of refuge", but many people came to us with stories of hurt, misunderstanding, and overly dominant leadership in their previous experiences. These actually seemed to be suffering from a kind of post-traumatic stress flowing out of a real toxicity from various experiences or backgrounds. While they wanted to find God, they were hindered by a fearfulness and the aftershocks of their experiences. In DBC they seemed to discover some solace, comfort, and grace. We discovered many who were shaking off effects of several very different backgrounds and trying to recover their faith in church life. While my desire is to be kind and fair, it seems prudent to me to attempt a survey of some of these backgrounds.

THE CATHOLIC ENVIRONMENT

The immediate area around DBC is generally acknowledged to be about two-thirds Roman Catholic or people who were at least raised in the Catholic church. How little did I understand this when we came to DBC in 1983! Catholicism has held a long and powerful cultural influence in Bristol County, Massachusetts, and while not all of that influence has been bad, there is a definite preconditioning that people possess. Many new attenders of DBC found themselves refreshed by the clearly "relaxed" way we do things, even in the earliest years of the church. Countless times I have heard people say that in coming *from* a Catholic background, they were invigorated to be encouraged to read the Bible for themselves, explore a personal (rather than an institutional) relationship with God, and discover some joy in the community life of the church (what we call "body life," a term we took from California pastor Ray Stedman, 1917–1992).

Working with people from a Catholic background has had an encouraging effect as well, in that they are already "on board" with certain aspects of theology: the idea of a holy God, the Ten Commandments, the Trinity, the reality of sin, the cross and substitutionary nature of Christ's death, the resurrection, etc. There has also been a strong affinity for family loyalty and indeed *many* large and well-connected families with whom to work. Our best church growth has come by seeing our people reaching their own family members. This was not a thing I saw as much in Washington, DC, southwest Virginia, or Texas, where Renée and I had also lived.

However, there is a real sense in which DBC (and other churches) has served as a "safe haven" from some of the more toxic or even abusive aspects of Catholicism. DBC provided an environment where people could ask questions—hard questions—about faith, life, the world around us, and social issues, without fear of condescension or shallow "just do what the church says" responses, to which many have said they were accustomed. Interestingly, many Catholic-raised people that we have met made their way to DBC as their *first* non-Catholic religious experience, positioning us with a unique responsibility. Our church has also offered a very unpretentious clergy-style in all of the pastors. People from a Catholic background have always found the style engaged by DBC's pastors to be refreshing in that regard. Finally, our church has helped people emerge from the fog and confusion of an overly formal and ritualistic way of "doing church", whether in Sunday-morning worship or all the other structures and traditions that come with Roman Catholicism.

THE LIBERAL PROTESTANT TRADITIONAL BACKDROP

On the other hand, some people who came to the DBC family derived from mainstream and theologically liberal Protestant church traditions—Congregational, Episcopal, Lutheran, Presbyterian, and Methodist. These traditions affected them with a more subtle kind of worldview and a lower confidence in the Scripture than that held by people raised in a Catholic tradition. But they were spiritually hungry and came to DBC with a curiosity about the Bible and somehow, a desire to unlearn the low view of Scripture taught in their church of upbringing. In this DBC served as a haven from doubt and an incubator of new spiritual possibilities and hope. Over the years, DBC has had little contact with the area's liberal interchurch affiliations, though they have had some evangelicals within their memberships.

Vineyard Christian Fellowship

With the beginning of the "Vineyard" in 1977, a collaborative church-planting effort between John Wimber and Kenn Gulliksen in Anaheim, California, a few DBC people began to move toward it. The Vineyard had a distinctively charismatic but theologically aware flavor. Many good theologians around the country were watching and studying it and commenting. When I arrived at DBC, this migration of some DBC people to the new local Vineyard was underway, and it felt like a threat to me as a young pastor. To be sure, I wanted as much of the Holy Spirit as there might be to have, but I was unmoved by the "hip" talk that accompanied Vineyard meetings and rallies. I was also skeptical of the genuineness of claims for miracles, "words" from the Lord, and the disorder of spontaneous worship. While I liked the idea of freshness and immediacy of the Lord's presence, I was not at all convinced that the Vineyard way was altogether trustworthy or up to its claims.

Aware that our church had lost some good people to the Vineyard, we watched their branch in New Bedford, which later moved to Dartmouth. The very founder of the term "Vineyard," Kenn Gulliksen, who had grown up in Dartmouth until the age of twelve, was dispatched to restart the church again after its initial collapse. I met with Kenn and found him to be a tremendously sincere and spiritual man. His ministry, however, lasted only two years but was then followed by an earnest twelve-year pastorate by Tad Blackburn and then a pastorate by music leader Richie Savino. The Vineyard finally closed in 2010. DBC received a few Vineyard faithful at that time, and Richie and Ruthie Savino remain good friends of DBC.

THE BIBLE SPEAKS AND ASSOCIATED CHURCHES

In 1986 The Bible Speaks network of churches, headquartered in Lenox, Massachusetts, and closely affiliated with Rev. Carl Stevens (1929–2008), became defunct. But after and before then, a couple of its affiliated churches in our region have left their impression on many people. Their ministries are widely publicized in the region, but DBC found itself receiving a number of people over the years who had spent time in these formerly The Bible Speaks churches. While the Christian Research Institute dubbed The Bible Speaks as a collective of ministries that freshly brought Christ and the gospel to many New Englanders in the 1960s and 70s when few others were, it was sad that often when those people came to us, they arrived in an injured or at least a very wary state.

In one particular case, a local church of TBS persuasion engendered a very high degree of loyalty among many of its members, but others have testified to a significant toxicity in church leadership practices. We have sought to understand the nature of that church's philosophy of ministry, and again, this has been confused by the fact that evidently The Bible Speaks churches are theologically evangelical in many of their core beliefs. While it has not at all been the spirit of our church to be "separatist" in general, DBC has not felt free to endorse or embrace these churches in any of their ministries in any noticeable way—though it grieves us to maintain this distance. Interestingly, Rev. Robert Pardon of the New England Institute for Religious Research, a very capable researcher in these things, has confirmed the aberrant nature of these churches in a studied analysis of their ministry.

SUPER-FUNDAMENTALIST CHURCHES

There have also been visitors to DBC who have come out of stridently fundamentalist churches. I almost do not want to use the term *"fundamentalist"* because in core doctrine, these churches are virtually equivalent to DBC. There is little disagreement as to the "fundamentals" of the evangelical faith and understanding of the Bible.[28] Fundamental*ism,* however, has come to include additional attitudes and convictions related to secondary affiliations, associations, and lifestyle standards that go beyond purely doctrinal and biblical considerations. One particular strand of connection deserves mention.

When my ministry in Dartmouth began, I sought out fellowship with the evangelical pastors I would hear about, or at least with the ones with whom I imagined I may share some solidarity. I have always enjoyed a collegial relationship with fellow pastors and ministers. One such pastor was Rev. Dean Bonsall at Calvary Bible Church in Westport. Pastor Bonsall was older, and we shared some fellowship until his retirement in 1991. He invited me to speak at Calvary on a couple of occasions, which I happily accommodated. His successor, Pastor Greg Gifford, became a good friend and enthusiastically helped me set up DIBS. His pastorate, however, terminated in just two years. Pastor Gifford and his family attended DBC for a time and then relocated to Ohio, where Greg and his wife, Carol, minister today. In the years that immediately followed, Calvary Bible Church sharply distanced themselves from DBC. It seems to me to be a great paradox that in fact, over the years no other single church has had more of an impact on DBC than has Calvary Bible Church. A number of people in DBC worshipped or ministered in Calvary at one time or another. Several were *raised* in Calvary Bible Church and marvelously learned the gospel there.

---

[28] *The Fundamentals* or *The Fundamentals: A Testimony To The Truth,* edited by A. C. Dixon and later by Reuben Archer Torrey, is a set of ninety essays in twelve volumes published from 1910 to 1915 by the Bible Institute of Los Angeles. They were designed to affirm orthodox Protestant beliefs, especially those of the Reformed tradition, and defend against ideas deemed inimical to them. They are widely considered to be the foundation of the modern Fundamentalist movement.

Sadly, though, a spirit of confusion and misunderstanding laced with some harshness appears to have grown internally there and precipitated an internal struggle within Calvary in 2001 and 2002 with a major departure of Calvary people on Easter Sunday of 2002. I was approached that Good Friday by a Calvary leader (though I did not know he was one) and informed that on that Easter Sunday, there would probably be "a dozen or so" Calvary people worshipping in DBC. Fifty-four Calvary people arrived that morning. I met with them in the week following and then sought out the CBC pastor (twice), seeking to facilitate or mediate a return to Calvary for them. He was a Bob Jones University graduate, as were other CBC leaders at the time. He seemed uninterested and unmoved at my approach, and they were unable to return, so sharp had been their conflict and so deep their injuries. Reconciliation was not to be.

The tragedy of this was highlighted in that some had been in Calvary for many years and others were but young believers. As stated before, and not without irony, the actual doctrine and theology of both churches were (and remain) virtually indistinguishable. DBC and Calvary Bible Church have shared a number of key leaders. Former DBC Pastor Mel Longtin came to DBC as pastor in 1976 from service as a deacon in Calvary Bible Church. Pastor Longtin's wife, Susan, grew up in Calvary. Current DBC elder Rev. Bill Stack was also a deacon in CBC and filled the pulpit there for several months in 1989. DBC people Debbie Donner, Victor Gonsalves, and Sallie Wilson were all raised in CBC. Bill Jr. and Hope Hallett worshipped and ministered in CBC for a number of years. Shirley Barboza remembers her baptism in the old Calvary Bible Church at Westport Factory. DBC began supporting a long-standing CBC missionary family that coincidentally CBC had dropped (in part at least because of a connection that missionary had with Dallas Theological Seminary's Spanish Doctor of Ministry program in Guatemala; a severance-of-support letter indicated this as the reason). The list of indirect and direct connections between DBC and CBC goes on, although none of the "cross pollination" or shared history has been conscious or deliberate. In recent times, I am gratified to have enjoyed congenial talks with Calvary's present pastor, who is a man of much graciousness and patience. The Lord is to be praised any time His fruit of love is present.

In the years that followed the event described above, DBC worked to enfold the people hurt in that struggle as well as receiving people from other super-fundamentalist churches. Between people from The Bible Speaks background, from CBC, and from even more aberrant backgrounds, and even recovering people damaged by cults, DBC came to feel a bit like a MASH unit![29] The flow of injured and confused Christians defined a chapter of our *own* history, as had the more pleasant merger with Elim ten years earlier. Somehow DBC has managed to avoid a super-fundamentalist flavor, although we are thoroughly evangelical and conservative in our understanding of Scripture, doctrine, and the "fundamentals" of the faith.

As a postscript, only about a dozen Calvary people eventually made a home at DBC and many drifted elsewhere (some to the small but new "Dartmouth Baptist Church," which had actually moved to New Bedford and itself is considering closing in 2012). This conflict was one of the saddest things I have seen in all my ministry, and we took no pleasure in receiving wounded people from a sister church. In the same few years though, we watched other church splits in far North Dartmouth and in Lakeville also occur, also within "sister" churches. Observing these troubles humbled us and drove us to prayer more fully.

INTERNATIONAL STUDENT MINISTRIES

We don't really believe in accidents, but it seems quite accidental (or at least not deliberate) that DBC has become in recent years a safe haven for many UMass Dartmouth graduate students and families

---

[29] MASH stands for mobile army surgical hospital.

who are international in origin. Much of this is due to the untiring effort and loving ministries of Rev. David and Ruth Schaffer—but it is to the credit of a number of other DBC people as well. To date, DBC has welcomed, assisted, and enfolded UMD (and otherwise associated) people from China, Taiwan, Vietnam, Ghana, Sierra Leone, Nigeria, Germany, Japan, England, India, Israel, Cameroon, Brazil, Ukraine and Haiti. Many stories could be cited to illustrate this outreach—and one deserves mention from my perspective!

In 2004 I received an e-mail from Kansas State University veterinary medicine Professor Robert Taussig. Professor Taussig contacted us (illustrating the value of internet networking) to let us know that a young Chinese PhD who had recently been hired by UMass Dartmouth would be soon moving to Dartmouth. Could we assist her? When Dr. June Jiao arrived with her son Ben, Renée assisted her to find an apartment in the town of Dartmouth, believing that Ben would do well in the Dartmouth school system. Renée located an apartment on the very edge of the Dartmouth town line! In subsequent years, as June worked for the School for Marine Science and Technology, Ben graduated as valedictorian from Dartmouth High School, excelled in the DHS band, and won a scholarship to Harvard University. June's husband, Dr. Wengang Che, and their younger son, Robert, also became much loved in DBC. Also in 2006 we had the happy chance to meet "Dr. Bob" Taussig and wife, Mary, when they briefly visited Massachusetts! In our home for one evening, Dr. Bob immediately grabbed up our new mini-poodle puppy, MacArthur, and gave him a thorough exam! Dr. Taussig went home to be with the Lord on May 21, 2012, one week short of his eighty-ninth birthday.

Previous to this time, in the early 1990s DBC co-hosted a Chinese New Year party for the Chinese Student Association of UMD. This was our first attempt to get to know some Chinese students and faculty from the university. What I remember is a conversation on the church's front porch between a student from Taiwan and one from mainland China. There was some tension between students from the two places, but these two were having a deliberate conversation fostering understanding and tolerance. I was thankful that we provided the location at least for such a conversation.

Developing a Culture of Balance

If there has been one overriding message I have received from the Lord, other than the urgency of the gospel, it is to seek and maintain a sense of balance in ministry. Many factors work to undermine this pursuit, but it has been noted by many who come into DBC that our church visibly values a culture of balance. Several arenas of contest, theological and practical, showcase the fight to sustain a balanced ministry.

Law and Grace

This is a classic set of opposites both in theology and in day-to-day Christian living. In DBC we have sought to emphasize grace but not to the detriment of promoting a biblical lifestyle. We try to shun legalism and give each Christian the freedom to "work out their own salvation with fear and trembling" (Phil.2:12) It has not been easy to maneuver between law and grace, as people will often lean one way or another. Are we "about" the free acceptance by God of sinners and the "come as you are" standard, or are we about being a place of respectability and protocol and dignity that is policed by the church leaders? Do we insist on everyone serving in some ministry, or do we enable people to attend church indefinitely and never approach them about serving? What about frequency of church attendance, tithing, use of alcohol, gambling, movie-watching, quiet before worship begins, attendance at business meetings, and an almost endless list of other questions? DBC has sought to feature "grace" while modeling the "law of Christ" (Gal. 6:2).

LIGHT-HEARTED, BUT NOT UNDIGNIFIED OR DISORDERLY

"Light-hearted with a serious love of God's Word" is what we have said on our church website. A church should certainly not be a place with a downcast or negative spirit about it. DBC has sought to strike a good balance between happiness and laughter and good boundaries about dignity. It hasn't always been easy to strike that balance. Our desire, though, has been to attempt to create a welcoming atmosphere that is inviting, especially to the hurting, and at the same time to emphasize the majesty and glory of the Lord.

NOT CHARISMATIC, BUT NOT ANTI-CHARISMATIC

We have wanted to be distinguished from those churches that have seemed to have an anti-charismatic attitude because distrust of those features too easily spills over into a mean-spirited criticism that goes beyond simple biblical evaluation of a doctrine. We also are cautious about having too absolute of a dogmatism regarding any providence the sovereign Spirit may or may not enact. At the same time, we have not wanted to be identified as a church that practices the charismatic "gifts" since we have developed our stated view of this. From the DBC Affirmation of Faith, there is this portion over which we labored for some time:

> Section 16: Spiritual Gifts
>
> We believe the Scriptures teach that all believers, since the beginning of the Church at Pentecost, have received at least one spiritual gift (1). These gifts are the result of the Holy Spirit baptizing the believer into the Body of Christ at the time of conversion, and correspond to the functions of members of the body (2). These gifts were given for the edification and good of the local Church and not the individual recipient alone (3), and should never be a source of fleshly pride or division (occurrences of which contradict the very purpose of Christ's Body). The

New Testament places the emphasis upon the Spirit-filled service to the Body and not primarily upon one's discovery of a spiritual gift.

We acknowledge that God is the sovereign Giver of gifts, and that He will bestow those enablements and abilities upon believers in accordance with His own counsel. Dartmouth Bible Church therefore recognizes, affirms and nurtures the following spiritual gifts (alphabetically listed): Administration/leading/government, encouragement, evangelism/missions, exhortation, faith, giving, helps, mercy, pastor-teacher, and teaching. Certain other gifts mentioned in the New Testament were used by God during the formation of the early church and during the completion of the N.T. These were never universal gifts nor can they be urged upon anyone. It is not the practice of our church to seek, employ or teach these kinds of gifts for public worship or ministry.

We also view that the gifts mentioned in the N.T. may not exhaust all the ways in which God may enable believers for ministry. He may also sovereignly bestow additional spiritual gifts not specifically mentioned in the N.T., and always with a view to the mutual edification of His Body, and the spread of the Gospel of Jesus Christ.[30]

ELDER FORM OF GOVERNMENT WITH STRONG CONGREGATIONAL INPUT

With the shift to an elder form of government, utilizing multiple men as a team for government, spiritual guidance, and shepherding, we did not want to lose a strong practice of congregational input for major decisions. DBC maintains a quarterly practice of an open meeting, works to develop and support as many teams for carrying out ministry

---

[30] This section was authored by myself and Robert Whitlow after much study and discussion.

as is practical, and at the same time deferring to the board of elders for any final ruling beyond the team level. The congregation votes on officers and the budget each year at the Annual Congregational Meeting and has input in any number of ways at other times. This, we hope, strikes a balance in decision making that does not lay all the responsibility on the elders or on the congregation.

BAPTIST WITH A SMALL B

If one must line DBC up with a denominational heritage, it would be with the Baptist movement. DBC is happily aligned at this time with Converge Worldwide, formerly known as the Baptist General Conference. The word *"Baptist"* was dropped from the church's title in 1981. However, the core doctrines that define historic Baptist churches did not change for DBC. DBC has retained its Baptist heritage while contemporizing some of its strategies, a balance move seen in many other churches around the country. Indeed, a recent listing of the ten most recent Converge Worldwide national church plants reveals *none* with the word *"Baptist"* in the church's name.[31]

CALVINISTIC WITH A SMALL C

As with the matter of being a Baptist church, DBC has downplayed being a Calvinistic church. It is not clear how the early pastors stood on this topic or most of the other early leaders. From 1983, however, most leaders have been at least moderately Calvinistic. It was not until the summer of 2011 that I formally taught about Calvinism (and then only in a small group). This is because, while I am strongly Calvinistic in my outlook, I have not wanted to make that perspective definitive of our reputation. The exception to this moderation has been on the doctrine of eternal security, which is explicitly stated in our Affirmation of Faith.

---

[31] *Point* magazine, Spring 2012, *Converge Worldwide.*

PREMILLENNIAL AND DISPENSATIONAL, BUT NOT EXTREME

DBC has always been premillennial in our eschatology (view of the end times). Our *Affirmation of Faith* has always identified us as dispensational as well, meaning belief in a pretribulational rapture, a literal tribulation, and a thousand-year millennial reign of Christ—based on a plain-meaning interpretation of Revelation 20, 1st Thessalonians 4, Matthew 24, etc. But I have found these theological tags to be unnecessarily schismatic and confusing to new Christians more often than not. Therefore, we have sought a balanced and controlled discussion of eschatology, even in one case in the hiring of an "amillennial" staff member. He agreed to not teach amillennialism while on the DBC staff, and it did not prove any difficulty.

BODY LIFE, BUT NOT TOO DECENTRALIZED

DBC, as most smaller churches, has enjoyed a "family feel" to our church life. Most attenders and members enjoy being *friends* with each other as well as fellow worshipers. We have sought to be more than associates and to simulate really being brothers and sisters. Ray Stedman published the book *Body Life* in 1972, and it is widely recognized as a classic on the subject of "authentic church." DBC has exploited many strategies to achieve a good sense of "body life" but hopefully not at the expense of an awareness of the wider body of Christ.

Imbalance can come with too much emphasis on small groups and no sense of a wider kinship or ownership of the whole body. Conversely, no involvement with small groups or teams or personal connection other than Sunday morning or "business" affiliation with the church misses much of the real blessing and richness of body life. DBC seeks and has sought a balance in the area of week-to-week church life and relationships between members.

ACCOUNTABILITY GROUPS, BUT NOT TOO CONTROLLING

Some in the body felt the need to become even closer to a trusted and select small group of Christian friends. Accountability came into vogue as a word for ministry during the Promise-Keepers years. A few small groups, mainly for men, began in DBC, as did one for married couples. Some of these groups last for "a season" and run their course; others last longer. The dangers of too much small-group accountability are an overbalance of control and possible loss of joy. Caution has been exercised to safeguard against too much control being exerted over members by virtue of their transparency and trust in small groups while providing meaningful connection and support for the Christian life.

ALL KINDS OF PEOPLE

It is hoped that DBC will always include a casual diversity of all kinds of people: older, younger, seekers, new Christians, disciple-makers, men, women, many children, teens, families, singles, people who are indigenous to Bristol County, people from other areas of the country, students, graduate students, people from any and all professions, international people, and many races. A church that includes multiple kinds of people is set up for a better balance in perspective and a better sense of how God is leading. This is something we seek as a church.

WHAT THE FUTURE HOLDS

Currently I am in the process of holding "roundtable" discussions with various DBC people toward envisioning the future of our church. What is the sense of how God might lead this congregation? What lessons from the past can inform the next generation about the life of the church and its ministry to the community? What will be the nature of a new generation of leadership, and what training for them can be set up now? What will be the scope of ministry and the specific areas targeted that DBC is equipped and gifted to address? I wish to discover what the *present* membership envisions or can imagine DBC will be like in ten and twenty years.

Our goal is not to pay tribute to traditions. It is, as was Chaloner Durfee's and the earliest members in 1963, to honor the Head of the church, the Lord Jesus Christ, in each and every church decision and endeavor and to handle accurately the Word of truth.

No church knows how long the Lord will bless its ministry; one would assume for as long as the Word of God is taught faithfully, the saints are equipped, love is experimental, and the lost are evangelized and discipled. As long as our church members and leadership seek the Savior's face, love His will, and long for His Kingdom, we can expect Him to use us. DBC humbly hopes our ministry will grow at exactly the pace with which the Lord Jesus Christ leads—no faster and no slower. It is unnecessary to apologize for wishing to reach many more people locally, regionally, and even internationally, with the good news of Jesus Christ. We cannot see what challenges or opportunities will unfold in the coming years. But we expect to discern the voice of the Lord and the leading of His Spirit, as we are dependent on those "signal" blessings from Him who is the Head of the church. May we be nothing but an honor to Him until He comes again.

ad Dei gloriam

Appendix 1

MISSIONARIES AND SUPPORTED MISSIONS ORGANIZATIONS

Names	Mission/Field	Years DBC Supported
John and Karen Ames	Baptist General Conference	1991–2002
Rick and Myla Berry	Converge Worldwide	2003–present
Frank Carmical	Harvester Ministries	2004–present
Walter Davenport	Overseas Christians Serviceman's Center	1968–74, 1981
Ken and Erma Gullman	BGC	1991–95
Martha Gushee	Indian Bible College	1987–89, 1997–present
Al and Jeanette Gustafson	BGC	1991–92
Rev. and Mrs. James Harding	AIM	1971–81, 84
Ken and Karen Hoffmeyer	Awana New England	1994–present
Matthew and Rebecca Litchfield	CRU—UMass Dartmouth	2012–present
Dr. Moses and Maria Mariscal	Hispanic missions and training	2008–present
Rev. and Mrs. Manuel Marques	Global Outreach	1968–1980

Bill and Katherine Martin	Converge Worldwide	2010–present
Steve and Debbie Meehan	Touch the World	2005–2010
John and Melissa Mitchell	Campus Crusade for Christ/ CRU	2005–2011
Tom and Melody Monk	TEAM	1990–1995
Dr. Dave and Jane Owen	BGC/NBC	1991–1995
Rev. Robert and Judy Pardon	New England Institute for Religious Research	1995–present
Rev. Whitney and Mimose Pierre	Converge Worldwide	2005–present
Rev. David and Ruth Schaffer	Community Chaplain Service	1987–present
Dr. Gary and Ruth Stephens	Converge Worldwide	1995–2012
Janet Thomson	WBT	2002–2009
Kevin and Ping Whitehead	Operation Mobilization/ Children's Hope	1988–2007
Baptist General Conference/Converge Worldwide		1968–81, 2002–present
Northeast Baptist Conference/Converge Northeast		1968–81, 1995–present
The Gideons	Local	Occasional
Radio Bible Class		1967–1980
DBC Windows to the World	DBC	2002–present
DBC Youth Missions trips	DBC	2004–present
DBC short-term missions	DBC	2002–present

Briefly Supported (less than three years)

Haje and Kelly Anderaus	Word of Life	1988
David and JoAnn Sullivan (Fall River)	Ireland	1988
Ken and Kathy Ashcroft	Italy	1987
Tom and Pat DeCosta	Lakeside Retreat Center (NBC)	1981
Rev. Robert D'Entremont	Regional	1977
Gary Dereshinsky	ABMJ	1987
Rev. Nathan and Eileen Hall	World Harvest (Ireland)	2003–2004
Dave and Evelyn Martin	Christian Camp (PA)	1981
Barrington College	Rhode Island	1968–1980
Camp Tispaquin	Northeast Baptist Conference	1967, 1971–72
Campus Crusade for Christ		1969
Christian School of Greater Fall River		1975–1981
Elim Park Baptist Home	Connecticut	1975–1981
Haven of Rest Mission		1975
Newport Bible School		1975
Open Doors		1984
The TEAM (Vinny Rideout)	New England	1984
World Vision		1984
Vancouver Bible College		1977

Appendix 2

DBC's Church Officers, 1963 to 2013

Elders (fifteen): Steuart Bailey Jr., Donald Clapp, Rev. Dr. Neil Damgaard, Thomas DeCosta, Brendan Gahan, William Hallett Jr., Paul Hsia, Dr. Larry Logan, Michael Martin, Louis Parascand Jr., Dr. Dean Schmidlin, Frank Sinclair, Rev. William Stack, Robert Whitlow, John Zarecki

Deacons/Deaconesses (seventy-eight): Brian Soldevilla, Dr. Roland Chan, Shirley Barboza, Kirsten Larsen, Liang Li, Carol Stack, Fran Theriault, Derek Thomas, Elizabeth Zarecki, Tom Saunders, Maureen Saunders, Jean Silva, Ron Silva, Barry Mingola, Jerry Sanders, Susan Sanders, Richard Setteducati, Donna Wingrove, Keith Constant, Normand Dufault, Jonathan Donner, Charlotte Hsia, Pauline Moniz, Danielle Perry, JoAnn Vangel, David Cadieux, John Zarecki, Tom Marginson, Paul Hsia, Bill Leite, Paul Souza, Betty Aanensen, Laura Duarte Crook, Madeline Sinclair, Steuart Bailey Jr., Jerry Corkum, Richard Halliwell, Ron Gallegos, Ray St. Don, James Tomasia, Michael Ponte, Robert Graham, Gene Demers, Robert Whitlow, Ron Brunette, Russell Viera, Donald Laprade, Michael Martin, Christine Martin, Thomas DeCosta, Patricia DeCosta, William Hallett Sr., William Hallett Jr., Cathy Burns, Susan Longtin, J. P. Smith, Roylene Smith, Carol Rose, Evelyn Martin, Elizabeth Russell, Ann Marie Allen, Fred Parlee,

Appendix 3

DBC Annual Budget Amounts, 1963 to 2012

YEAR	BUDGET	CHANGE	NOTES
2012	$317,200.00	3.38%	17.3% for Missions
2011	$306,800.00	3.61%	
2010	$296,088.00	-0.002%	
2009	$296,660.00	1.16%	
2008	$291,980.00	-4.35%	
2007	$305,240.00	5.97%	
2006	$288,055.00	9.78%	
2005	$262,392.00	5.34%	
2004	$249,080.00	5.04%	
2003	$237,120.00	32.20%	Major numerical growth
2002	$179,400.00	42.30%	Major numerical growth

YEAR	BUDGET	CHANGE	NOTES
1987	$31,791.67	6.02%	
1986	$29,984.14	-12.40%	
1985	$34,236.56	10.62%	3% for Missions
1984	$30,948.80	25.52%	
1983	$24,655.83	-27.30%	Pastoral transition
1982	$34,111.80	22.55%	No Pastor
1981	$27,834.80	35.74%	No Pastor
1980	$20,506.30	10.22%	No Pastor
1979	$18,604.60	21.43%	
1978	$15,321.50	25.00%	
1977	$12,258.30	37.93%	

YEAR	BUDGET	CHANGE	NOTES
2001	$126,100.00	5.43%	
2000	$119,600.00	4.55%	
1999	$114,400.00	8.21%	Construction year
1998	$105,716.00	2.16%	
1997	$103,480.00	32.67%	
1996	$78,000.00	-1.89%	
1995	$79,500.00	-4.45%	
1994	$83,200.00	-5.89%	
1993	$88,400.00	0.00%	
1992	$88,400.00	-1.45%	

YEAR	BUDGET	CHANGE	NOTES
1976	$11,810.30	20.03%	Pastoral transition
1975	$9,839.30	32.85%	Pastoral transition
1974	$7,406.30	23.41%	
1973	$6,001.30	1.83%	Pastoral transition
1972	$5,990.30	17.27%	
1971	$5,108.45	-18.98%	Pastoral transition
1970	$6,304.80	6.31%	
1969	$5,930.80	300.10%	
1968	$1,973.00	5.34%	
1967	$1,873.00	44.08%	

YEAR	BUDGET	CHANGE	NOTES
1991	$89,702.56	206.10%	Merger with Elim
1990	$43,516.56	4.79%	
1989	$41,526.56	12.15%	
1988	$37,027.47	16.47%	

YEAR	BUDGET	CHANGE	NOTES
1966	$1,300.00	14.14%	
1965	$1,139.00	242.86%	
1964	$469.00		Pastor's death
1963	$986.28		

Appendix 4

DBC Baptisms, 2000–2012

Feb 2000		Feb 2005		Sept 2008	
	Paul Demers		"Alex" Tzuu-Wang Chang (UMD)		Alicia Sullivan
	Paul Ferreira		Heather Contant (UMD)		Lynn Brown
	Ana Ferreira		Aaron Donner		Jacqueline Rebello
	Kevin Medeiros		James Rees (UMD)		Elaine Medeiros
July 2000	Jared Sequeira	**June 2005**			Claudette Fontaine
			Fae Williams		Nicole Bailey with Steuart
	Keith Constant		Patrick Lannan		Rebekah Bailey with Steuart
Dec 2005	Tatum Constant		Vania Corkum	**Mar 2009**	
	Garwood "Red" Faunce				Sophia Freeman with Jacob
	Shawn Perry		Renée Cafarella		Marina Guo
	Danielle Perry		Nichole Ellis	**Sept 2009**	
	Wayne Souza		Gretchen Houseman (UMD)		Glenn Chamberlain

195

Dec 2000			Christine Laventure		Mark Jones
	Jason Corkum		Fran Logan		Chris Rose
	Russell Teasdale Sr.		Robyn Mazo		Dr. Yu Zhou (UMD)
	Russell Teasdale Jr.	**Sept 2006**		**Jan 2010**	Alex Chery (UMD)
Feb 2002	Rachel Donner		Louis Medeiros		Dwight Cheetham
	Matthew Hebert		Brittini Sousa		Chris Falkowski
	Jerry Sanders	**Dec 2006**			Theresa Milner
	Susan Sanders		Leia Brunette		Phil Norton
Aug 2003			J.J. Hartley (UMD)	**Sept 2010**	(Saunders' Home)
	Aubrey Constant		Megan Hsia		Mathew Vangel
	Paul Roy		Bob Saunders		Elyse Gonsalves
Dec 2003			Jamie Tarricone	**Mar 2011**	
	Tuesday Bethoney		Alexander Zarecki		April Clay
	Wanda Dow	**Oct 2007**			"Richard" Chun Liu

Megan Whitlow	Kathy Baptiste with Brian	Joshua Cosmo
Mar 2004	Valerie Burke	Lacey Lebert
Barbara Grenier	Katherine Bethoney	**Jan 2012**
Cory Durfee	Fernanda Johnson	Lisa Chan
Benjamin Durfee	Sergio Mazo	Eric Meilert
Dominic Zarecki	Bob Mello	Jennifer Modzelewski
	Hannah Larsen	

Appendix 5

MISCELLANEOUS MEMORABILIA

We are pleased to display the seal of the American Camping Association for the first time. After a careful check on program and grounds we are recognized as acceptable and worthy of merit implied by the Seal.

On Tispaquin Pond—Middleboro, Mass.
Owned and Operated By
Baptist General Conference of N. E.

Northeast Baptist Conference Camp 1963

Dartmouth builds a   church.

Students today are seeking for fulfillment in many areas of their lives. They are groping for spiritual enlightenment and many are searching in the wrong directions. A generation in revolt, today's students nevertheless look for a positive foundation for their beliefs.

In our OPPORTUNITY this month we can help a new church to gain a foothold in the community before an influx of students comes within reach of its ministry. The only answer to their turmoil and unrest is Jesus Christ.

Dartmouth Baptist Church in North Dartmouth, Massachusetts, owns a corner lot just one block from the new Southeastern Massachusetts Technological Institute. While the college will not be completed till 1972, the Dartmouth church will be ready for occupancy this spring.

This will give the church an opportunity to establish a broad outreach to meet the spiritual needs of a growing student body.

The coming of the college will mean the certain expansion of the town as people move in to provide the increasing necessities of life. The jobs created by such a society will give permanence and stability to families. Dartmouth church stands ready to serve them. Their attractive sanctuary will welcome the established citizen of the community as well as the new families who are looking for a church home.

In 1963 a small group of believers met in a home for their first service. They soon outgrew the confines of a home and moved to the Veterans of Foreign Wars' Hall where they will meet until their new sanctuary is ready.

The church called Rev. James Harding to be its pastor in 1964.

That same year their church property was purchased. Final payment was made 12 months later. They joined the Baptist General Conference in 1965.

Construction on a church building began in October 1967. With deep trust in God the 19 members took on a $35,000 mortgage. Assuming such a responsibility is a monumental step of faith. It will require much sacrifice on the part of these people to meet the needs. They have agreed to provide labor on much of the inside work such as painting and laying tile. The added expense of these materials not provided for in the construction contract must be met by them, too.

OPPORTUNITY members are privileged to give the help that will strengthen the courage and faith of Dartmouth church. Sacrificial gifts to match what they are giving will give inspiration as they forge ahead.

The people at Dartmouth are aware of the great areas of service which are opening to them. They anticipate eagerly the ministry that they can have to the many, both permanent and transient, who must be reached for Christ.

The cost of revolt is astronomical!

March 1968   Call #155

Opportunity
BOARD OF HOME MISSIONS
BAPTIST GENERAL CONFERENCE
5750 NORTH ASHLAND AVENUE
CHICAGO, ILLINOIS 60626

- TO STOP
A REVOLT!

DBC Brochure 1968